SMALL TALK

Talk to Anybody in Any Situation With Complete Confidence

(How to Make Small Talk in Any Situation)

Phyllis Feldman

Published By Phyllis Feldman

Phyllis Feldman

All Rights Reserved

Small Talk: Talk to Anybody in Any Situation With Complete Confidence (How to Make Small Talk in Any Situation)

ISBN 978-1-77485-382-5

All rights reserved. No part of this guide may be reproduced in any form without permission in writing from the publisher except in the case of brief quotations embodied in critical articles or reviews.

Legal & Disclaimer

The information contained in this book is not designed to replace or take the place of any form of medicine or professional medical advice. The information in this book has been provided for educational and entertainment purposes only.

The information contained in this book has been compiled from sources deemed reliable, and it is accurate to the best of the Author's knowledge; however, the Author cannot guarantee its accuracy and validity and cannot be held liable for any errors or omissions. Changes are periodically made to this book. You must consult your doctor or get professional medical advice before using any of the suggested remedies, techniques, or information in this book.

Upon using the information contained in this book, you agree to hold harmless the Author from and against any damages, costs, and expenses, including any legal fees potentially resulting from the application of any of the information provided by this guide. This disclaimer applies to any damages or injury caused by the use and application, whether directly or indirectly, of any advice or information presented, whether for breach of contract, tort, negligence, personal injury, criminal intent, or under any other cause of action.

You agree to accept all risks of using the information presented inside this book. You need to consult a professional medical practitioner in order to ensure you are both able and healthy enough to participate in this program.

TABLE OF CONTENTS

INTRODUCTION 1

CHAPTER 1: CONVERSATIONAL SKILLS AND THEIR IMPORTANCE 3

CHAPTER 2: THE RELEVANCE OF SMALL TALK 7

CHAPTER 3: THE BENEFITS OF SMALL TALKS IN YOUR SOCIAL AND PERSONAL RELATIONSHIPS 15

CHAPTER 4: FINDING COMMON GROUND 25

CHAPTER 5: WHAT YOU CAN DO TO BUILD YOUR PEOPLE SKILLS 32

CHAPTER 6: UNDERSTANDING SMALL TALK 44

CHAPTER 7: THE BEST WAY TO ENGAGE IN SMALL TALK THE DO'S AND DON'TS 52

CHAPTER 8: MINIMAL TALK IN A VARIETY OF SITUATIONS 69

CHAPTER 9: TALKING TO SMALL PEOPLE FOR PEOPLE WITH SOCIAL ANXIETY 93

CHAPTER 10: WHAT TO BEGIN A CONVERSATION 103

CHAPTER 11: TIPS TO BE CONFIDENT WHEN TALKING TO STRANGERS 123

CHAPTER 12: GET OUT AND ENJOY THE DAY 143

CHAPTER 13: THE BEST WAYS TO CONNECT WITH ANYONE 147

CHAPTER 14: WHAT TO DO TO CLOSE A CONVERSATION POSITIVELY 172

CHAPTER 15: THE WAY TO LEAVE 'THE PARTY' 175

CONCLUSION 183

Introduction

All conversations begin with a small. Most often the conversation begins in a casual greeting and occasionally ends with a simple greeting, too. The greeting is simple however, the difficulty lies in how to make the smallest conversations last longer.

The ability to expand your circle of friends will help you greatly in your relationships, business and at work. It also helps to create new connections and provide opportunities to progress within your career.

It is said that you have to have lots of charisma in order to make even small conversations into memorable ones. If you lack charisma, your conversation likely to be a failure. This is totally false.

Charisma can only help you communicate quickly with others. It's just that sugary coating. What helps the conversation to grow is your ability to add something of substance to the conversation. It is possible to do this by learning more as well as paying attention and using body language correctly and enhancing your coping skills.

This book will guide you through the tried and tested methods and steps to make your conversation more productive by tackling the various kinds of conversationalists and concluding your conversation, leaving the other person interested in engaging with you again.

Chapter 1: Conversational Skills and their importance

Conversations are a crucial aspect to our everyday lives. It's nearly impossible to form a bond with anyone without having a conversation with one another. The ability to converse is vital since it is the most efficient way to express one's thoughts and thoughts.

Conversational skills do not just comprise speaking abilities as well as listening abilities. The conversation is always a multi-directional exchange. Being able to converse effectively means that you are able to be aware of when and when to talk and also the best time and manner to listen. This chapter will teach those who read this chapter the value of possessing excellent conversational skills.

Conversation with others is the most efficient method to disseminate information. Although it is possible to convey certain things using non-verbal communication however, the ability to express something to someone in a clear way is more effective. A good communication skills will allow you to communicate your thoughts with others in a relaxed manner.

Conversations help make to make a relationship grow. Whatever type of relationship you have with someone the bond between you will be more enduring if you engage in regular conversations periodically. For instance, a couple cannot keep their relationship going in the event that they are incapable of resolving conflicts through speaking to one another. In reality, the absence of interaction is the primary cause of relationships failing.

Good conversational skills aid in building the trust of others. If you're a professional in your communication abilities, people will have much less trouble talking with you and eventually will begin to be able to trust your abilities. In the end, having excellent communication skills will increase your credibility.

Conversational skills are beneficial in your professional career. Employers are now considering the ability to converse as a part of a candidate's skills. The candidates who are more conversant are more likely to be hired over those who can't. This is due to the fact that conversation is crucial in transactions, particularly in the field of business. In fact, in the majority of companies good communication skills are essential for top positions. Being able to communicate effectively can assist you in establishing a positive future.

These are only a few examples of many motives having excellent conversational skills is essential. Being able to communicate effectively isn't only a requirement however, it is also a privilege. It is not common for people to be born with excellent communication skills, but they can improve their skills with time. The following chapters in this book will offer you some tricks to improve your the art of conversation.

Chapter 2: The Relevance of Small Talk

There was a period when people would wait eagerly to talk with friends and to socialize. There were no cellphones or computers to act as distractions. Small talk was an important aspect of life and it was a way to ensure that all members of the community had a great relationship with one another.

The small talk of today is no longer relevant. Thanks to the advances in technology we have accessibility to smartphones as well as other personal devices for communication, that allow them to communicate as well as send email. This prevents them from engaging in private conversations, and can create an era of separation between them. It is crucial to revive the habit of talking to each other and talking to strangers to increase our social circle.

To highlight its many advantages, I've shed details about its numerous advantages , and I also look at some of its drawbacks.

The benefits of small talk

Community feeling

Small talk is a great way to foster an atmosphere of belonging. It brings together different individuals in society and blurs the distinctions between them. People start to make friends with everyone around them and get to know their neighbors more effectively. The whole community begins to become one large family, and they start to respect one another. Conversations with friends can assist strangers to become part of the group and make them feel less uncomfortable. A variety of social taboos could be addressed collectively and thrown out. As time passes, a single individual will be able to join with others, and eventually have an extensive network of contacts.

Acceptance

If we are always in conversation with those who we know, then we'll become used to their behavior. We won't be able to build an extended network of friends and become more tolerant of individuals who behave differently. We'll be trying to avoid those who behave differently and become angry and annoyed by them.

The most effective solution is to engage in conversation with strangers, and then to begin accepting them for what they are. This will allow us to accept different types of behaviours and will also broaden our social circle. There are many kinds of people, and we can create an as diverse group of friends as we wish.

Create interest

Small talk can allow you find interesting conversations and keep you entertained. Through small-talk it is easy to be entertained and see it as an effective way to boost your brain's energy. It is common for us to get bored talking to the same group of people, and we want to find a different perspectives in our lives. Through small talk we can spark an interest in a different way and have an enjoyable time discussing the different topics of our interest and increase our knowledge.

Rekindle old bonds

There are times when we can lose contact with our closest acquaintances. We often drift away and cease to talk to them. We often long for their company, and try to get in touch with them once more.

If you've had a close relationship with an individual and now have separated, conversation is your most effective method to reconnect. It's not enough to begin with a large conversation to win someone back. You must start with a small amount and begin with basic conversations. It is possible to start with basic questions like "Hi I've been away for since a while and how are youdoing?" Then, you can continue to build upon the conversation, and gradually increase the size of the conversation.

Important to turn

Through small conversations You can transform into someone important. You can engage in meaningful conversations and connect with people around you. This will make you famous and turn you into an influential person. People will approach you with questions and issues and you will become a common person. This will boost confidence and you'll turn into an exuberant person who is appreciated and loved by everyone.

Network is better

Through your conversational skills you'll be able to build an extensive network of contacts and a vast acquaintance base. You will be able to interact with people and begin to classify them into various types. You will be able to judge and talk to someone based on looking at the way they look and their speech.

The small talk you have with your friends will allow you not only grow your network but also give you access to a variety of people from every aspect of life.

We can all learn from each other.

When you hold small conversations with people from different backgrounds and you'll be able to encourage each other to discuss about various aspects of life. You'll be able talk for hours and be able to motivate one another by sharing the stories of your lives. You'll start drawing inspiration from your small conversations, which eventually become a vast library of ideas.

Alongside the many advantages, small talk comes with a few drawbacks as they are listed under:

The disadvantages of small-talk

Time-consuming

While the length of small-sized talks will be brief and take less time however, getting used to small talk takes a significant amount of time. It's not possible to, suddenly begin small conversations with strangers. You must consider the issue and decide who you'd like to speak with. It is not possible to pick random strangers in the streets and begin talking to them. It is best to begin by talking to your friends of friends or colleagues working in your office but haven't spoken to or even met. This will take time and also require some effort. Additionally, you will need to do some study.

Confidence

While it is not necessary to have confidence in yourself to engage in conversation with others but most people be affected by a lack of confidence and fear of approaching strangers. Strangers can be intimidating and attempting to engage them in an exchange of words can be intimidating. More than the anxiety about approaching strangers It is the worry of not getting an answer and then having to face embarrassment that makes people avoid small-talk in any form.

Digital media

The rapid development of digital media is making people to lose desire to engage in conversation. There are movies and TV shows widely available and many people aren't keen to meet and socialize. They believe it is an extremely difficult task to get out of their homes and speak to strangers and prefer to contact them at home, while watching television as well as listening to the music, etc.

Chapter 3: The Benefits of Small Talks in Your Social and Personal Relationships

Small talk can greatly contribution to strengthening your personal relationships. This is not only about the romantic ones, but ones you make with your family, friends and people you've recently met, as well as other significant people that you interact with. Some people may see conversations with friends as trivial however, it plays a an important role in strengthening your relationships. It is an act of bonding. It's a great method to reduce the distance between people.

Small talk can also serve different purposes, helping people establish connections between family members, friends and new acquaintances, colleagues and so on. In particular it allows for friends to discover and define the social classification of one another. Additionally, it is connected to the demands and standards that are set by individuals to maintain the highest standards.

The benefit of small-sized talks is that it allows the person who starts it to feel accepted and loved every when they see that someone actually gets to hear them. Social interactions are facilitated in a more flexible way. However, the conclusion depends on the exact stage of conversation when small conversations begin.

Small talk is an important element of your personal as well as social relationships because it gives you the opportunity to make connections with people. If you look back and look back to see what you did to create an acquaintance or a non-familiar one and you'll most likely find the answer in small conversations. Engaging in it in a constructive manner helps to make your life easier and more focused on the success you want to achieve.

Be aware that you won't be able to predict who you'll see next. Every time you encounter someone new, you are able to make use of the ability to begin an informal conversation to establish an appropriate structure and a foundation for conversation. Through this, you could give them enough space to express your ideas in a pleasant manner.

Other possible reasons for why small talk is so valuable for both your social and personal relationships include:

It is an essential building block to build a Personal Connection

Humans are naturally drawn to be noticed and heard. This double recognition promotes harmony, respect and unity which are crucial to creating relationships. Small talk is powerful enough to open doors to interaction. They allow you to invite someone to join in the interaction in an more warm and non-threatening manner. It allows you to initiate informal and casual conversations which are thought to be beneficial to let those close to you know how friendly and interesting you are.

Small conversations can be talking about lighthearted remarks and asking questions. However, these basic actions can make the person you're speaking to feel that you're eager to communicate and connect. If you can initiate the conversation correctly and effectively, you'll be able to make him feel relaxed which will make him more open to your conversation.

It also acts as an element of a long-lasting connection as it connects people right now. You might only have had contact for a couple of minutes however that is enough to make a good first impression. This could spark the desire to to know one another more. It's possible that It could turn out to be the catalyst to establishing an ongoing relationship which you'll always be grateful for.

Eases Transition

Another benefit of having small conversations within your social and personal interactions is that they give you the ability to change effortlessly between roles - whether professional or personal. This makes it easier to changing roles. Your friendly and warm words could lead to a stronger personal connection. It can be a major factor to build trust and familiarity between individuals.

If you're in the middle of an argument that is heated or a debate it is also possible to use small talk to break the frozen ice. It's a great aid in bringing the mood back to a more peaceful one. Through small talk it becomes easy to remember that taking the time returning to your peaceful and tranquil environment often can restore your confidence. It helps ease transitions and is beneficial for resolving conflicts.

Begins to Form a More Deep Relationship

You will no longer view small talk as something that isn't important when you understand how crucial it is in the development of deep relationships. Be aware that it is impossible to expect strong and deep relationships to be formed without starting from small, casual conversations. Remember that they serve as the source of social interactions. Every great love story begins with small conversations. Same goes in business transactions that have been successful.

The most important thing is learning how you can communicate with other people, rather than simply communicating with them. Look for common areas that could be excellent conversations starting points. It might be as insignificant as the long line or the pleasant weather. This will be enough to create bonds that are most likely to endure for an extended period of time.

Can be used as a distraction during Tough Times

If you're facing a stressful circumstance, you'll most likely wish to get away from it for a short time. That's where conversations with your family members and your closest acquaintances can be helpful. You've already established relationships with them, and by keeping conversations casual it will help you get through the most difficult times. One of the main reasons you establish and maintain an individual relationship is that you'd like to have someone to help you through difficult moments.

Through small conversations it is possible to make and keep the bridge. It doesn't require you to break through any communication barriers. For example, if someone close to you is grieving due to the tragic loss of a loved one they're likely to be averse to the thought of discussing plans for a trip planned for next week. If he's willing to engage in conversations, you could simply ask questions or even talk about your life instead.

You can provide him with a few details of your personal life. This will make him forget the pain he's experiencing for a brief period. By having small and gentle conversations you can help him distract from the difficult situation he's currently in, creating a deeper bond.

Opens Up your Eyes

Another advantage of small talk is that it helps open you to world surrounding you. This is advantageous in your social and personal relationships. These talks can help to inform you about the current. This helps you increase your vigilance and awareness. This gives you the chance to be attentive to the world that are happening around you. By engaging in small discussions it is no longer necessary to be restricted to your mobile or other devices. It lets you see the need for other people being heard. You'll know when is the right moment to connect and communicate with one another.

Acts as a Conversation Starter

If you started small conversations with a stranger, it might make both people realize both are in good company. What you both require is a form of positive interactions. If you're in the course of a meeting, for instance it helps participants build a reputation and show off their talents and knowledge. If it's a brief discussion initiated by strangers it can be an opportunity to introduce themselves prior to engage in more practical discussions.

The great thing about this method is that it allows you feel your friend's mood. speaking to. You can also indicate your own personality, helping to create an effective connection. It allows you to leave a lasting impression. You can give information in the shortest amount of time , while aiding in assessing the environment. It's easier to study the landscape and sort things out, like the humor of the other person and sensibility. This is the most important aspect in creating a lasting impression.

Makes you Happy

It's possible to think this is a strange benefit but it's really the truth; even small talks can boost your happiness. If you speak to strangers and witness their calming smiles and gestures and you be more optimistic about yourself, which will make you feel more content. It is possible to expect that happiness to last for a long time if the conversation you started was able to turn into a friendly conversation and even a more bonded relationship, one that you could keep throughout your life.

Chapter 4: Finding Common Ground

If you've got an understanding of the term small talk and know the reason why it's crucial to develop a strong conversational foundation of this kind We're going take a look at the very first tip for small talk in this book. It's how to strike a chord with someone you do not really know. This is an excellent first step because it will help you understand the kinds of topics to stay clear of and avoid when seeking to have a general small talking success. Let's look at the various strategies can be used to discover an agreement with someone you're not sure of.

The Weather

One of the most popular topics to discuss with a stranger can be weather. Although it may seem to be a natural topic but the weather can be an excellent way to kick off an exchange and get started talking with anyone. One reason it is simple to discuss is the fact that it's an issue that both sides of the conversation can identify and to which they can both connect. Although discussing the weather may not be all that exciting, it can bring the conversation to life and let you discuss something you can identify with while you consider other topics to talk about. Below, you'll find a few words you could utilize if you're looking to discuss weather issues with someone else but don't have a clue where to start:

When the conditions are dull:

"It sure it would be nice to be somewhere else in Hawaii rather than here isn't it?"

When the weather's pleasant:

"We could not have had more pleasant a day had we had asked for it, would we?"

If it's raining:

I've heard there's going to be rain all weekend. Do you like storms?"

These are only suggestions. If you know an improved way of asking the questions, then you're well ahead. When you ask questions, it's likely that you'll be able to start an exchange of ideas, since the person you ask will be pressured to reply.

Mutual Friends

If you don't like discussing weather issues do not! Another way you could start a conversation without having to start a conversation about the weather is to discuss someone you know that two of you have in common. This tactic will only work in the event that you know the other person is in a relationship with one with whom you're also familiar, so be sure you are aware of this before you engage in this kind of conversation. A few ways to start the conversation include:

"So how do you find out about the _____ (Insert name)?"

"I have met _____ (Insert Name) when we were at school together. What was the way you met the person you met?"

"Isn't the _____ (Insert the name) the best?"

Possession Items

If the person you're talking has an item in their possession that's interesting to you, why not discuss it? This could include dogs, books babies, toys, or anything that you're carrying around at the moment. For instance, if you're in the store for groceries and you meet someone you're friends but don't really know it is possible to talk with them about the groceries that are in their cart , or the food they're planning to purchase in a specific aisle. As we've seen during the last chapter small talk is , by definition, spontaneous, meaning that you are free to discuss any topic that could result in a frank and open conversation. A few examples of conversation that are in use include the following types of questions:

"How do you know how old your child is?"

"What kind of breed do you have for your pet? I have a dog too!"

"What are your thoughts about this novel so far? I've been wanting to get it."

Common Experiments

If you are aware that the person you're talking to has probably been through similar experiences to your personal one, this is another excellent opportunity to engage in small-talk conversations. For instance, if your child plays involved in a sport and the process of registering during the time of season is extremely difficult or time-consuming for a reason, it's a good idea to discuss the issue with someone else who likely had a similar event. If you've recently been someplace, you could inquire with the person about whether they've visited the same area or even an entirely new location you can talk about with the person. Television shows can be an excellent method to spark a lively conversations with people. A few of the questions you can ask about to experiences that are common include the following:

"Do have you seen the most recent episode of this show? It was amazing wasn't it?"

"Have you ever been to _____ (name the location)? I went recently and it was amazing!"

"Did you attend that PTA session last Wednesday? It was brutal!"

After you've read through this section, you'll already have a number of strategies can be employed to bring the person into a position that makes them feel like you have something in common. People are naturally drawn to feeling that they're communicating with one who "gets" their feelings, so when you put your focus in obtaining a common experience from someone then you'll be able communicate with them better. The last thing you need to do is provide you with information about how engaging in conversation isn't without some imagination. Be prepared to be a bit eccentric or to be hesitant to ask multiple questions until you find one that sticks and is worthy of discussing.

Chapter 5: What You Can Do to Build Your People Skills

Like everyone else does it, you'll need to communicate with people in various ways throughout your life. The ability to communicate is essential in any kind of interaction regardless of whether it's shopping and making new friends, or leading a group. You're probably aware that the ability to communicate is for achievement. You've likely also realized that some methods of communication are superior to others. If you're looking to improve your interpersonal or people skills capabilities, you'll need to improve your image and your ways of interaction along with your verbal communications.

Learn What Makes Non-Verbal Communication

Non-verbal communication as the title implies, refers to everything that isn't to be related to the words you say. It could include the way you move your hands, what your facial expressions resemble and the way you sound. In this regard the majority of people depend on visual signals than on audio cues , and as such visual cues are more important to interpreting effectively. When it comes to visual cues people are more likely to glance at facial expressions instead of body language to understand the message you want to communicate.

If, for instance, you're trying to express the feeling of happiness, smiling is better than a speedier rate of speaking or an exuberant body language. Also, concealing your facial expression can make it easier to conceal how you're feeling at that moment, especially if you don't wish to reveal it, for instance, if you're scared of something, for instance.

Recognize the importance of non-verbal communication Is

Non-verbal communication should comprise approximately 60% of the interactions. To ensure the non-verbal communications you use works you must be able communicate your feelings in a way that other people can easily recognize.

It is important to pay attention to the non-verbal signals that you use when communicating. While doing this, consider the non-verbal signals that you are receiving from others and consider the information you get from these signals.

Master Body Language that makes others feel comfortable

The form of body language that puts people at ease differs from one culture to another. To make this book, I'll talk of Western culture. Your face and body must be directed toward the person you are talking to while you lean forward little toward them. It is also possible to employ gestures as well as variations in the volume or vocal rate, as well as facial expressions to convey your emotions. Make sure you listen attentively through smiling and nodding your head at the words they speak and, more importantly making sure you don't interrupt. Be alert , but relaxed as well.

That means your shoulders must be straight and your muscles need to be at ease. Also when you notice that you're focused too much on the way you look, concentrate on what the person in front of you is saying instead.

Differential Cultural Perspectives

Be aware that body language doesn't behave the same way across different cultures. What is considered to be a gesture to show respect within one society may be considered to be offending in another. One example is of burping. In Western society, burping in any form is considered rude and can even be considered offensive. But in certain

Middle-Eastern traditions, if one do not burp after eating it's considered to be as a serious disrespect to the host because it suggests that you didn't take pleasure in the meal.

Naturally, the non-verbal signals of the culture you're part of will be innate to you. But, if you are required to communicate with a culture different from your own take a look at others and determine what the most common non-verbal signals are. It might be helpful to learn more about these clues.

Examine the ways in which gender differences impact Non-Verbal Communication

When trying to comprehend and interpret non-verbal messages One of the aspects to be considered is the gender difference. The non-verbal signals are presented different by women and men. It is generally believed that women are thought as being more likely look at each other and smile, as well as be more open to touching regardless of whether they are giving as well as receiving. They also pay attention more, interrupt less often and can read facial expressions better than males are able to.

Be aware of your emotional cues

To be able to communicate effectively you need to be able to control the emotional signals that you exhibit. This is especially crucial when you're experiencing intense emotions. When you are in this state it's important to take a deep breath and attempt to locate a calm place. If you're sending tension-inducing signals using the body, attempt relaxing your language. Do not clench your fists, and ease your muscles as well as your jaw. Research has shown that people who manage and control their emotional signals will be more likely earn confidence from others.

Set goals

Check your conversations and determine the extent to which they have brought you the desired results. Examine whether you achieved your goal during that discussion. Are you confident that the other person was able to understand you and what you desired? If the answer is the negative, you'll have to plan your ability to communicate.

Persuade, not order Logic can be a effective tool to use when trying to convince someone else to take action. For instance, if you would like to convince your roommate to empty the trash this timearound, you could mention that, in order for you both to accomplish exactly the same work the other has to empty the trash the same way the same way you did the previous time.

Your body language should be warm and welcoming: If you think that your response to a question is not positive, try using a more your body language in a manner that is open as we have mentioned earlier. Try active listening as well.

Listen, but don't dominate the conversation. Pay attention to your response and how you interact with each other. Utilize verbal cues like "mmhmm", "really" and "go on" to signal that you're paying attention.

Be assertive however, in a strategically method Utilize 'I' based messages, not you-based messages. Instead of speaking in a threatening manner such as "You are making me angry, ..." Try using an assertive statement like "I'm experiencing a sense of anger ..."

Effective Communication is the key to success

Avoid using complicated and incoherent messages when a simple , direct message is sufficient. Make sure you plan and practice the message you want to convey as often as you are able to. This will ensure that your message will be delivered quickly and efficiently. A good communication skill doesn't only enable others to understand the message you intend to convey but also permit you to convey more information within the timeframe you want to.

If, for instance, you'd like to request someone to help your needs, you shouldn't beat around the bush. Instead of saying "If you feel it's appropriate and you have time could you agree to help me" ask, "Could you please do this for me?"

Let's Talk

Everyone wants to participate in conversation. You must be able to tolerate silences lasting only for a short period of time to allow people to speak. One of the hallmarks of a good speaker is their ability to concentrate on the person they are talking with.

Try noticing how long you've been speaking in a specific conversation. If you've been talking about your words for a long time you can wrap it up, then stop talking so that the other person is aware when it's their turn to speak.

Know What Makes a an effective conversation

Effective communication is built on five pillars: relevancy to the audience, accuracy modesty, politeness and relevance. It is assumed that the speech will accomplish at least one things like:

Add new and previously undiscovered details previously unknown

Add aspects that are relevant and interesting

You can be honest, as long as you make use of devices like irony or sarcasm

Please be courteous

Do not be cocky and boastful.

Don't make assumptions or assume things

A clear and concise communication can avoid any miscommunication. Assumptions and assumptions can obscure the message and ruin your relationships. For example, if an old requests you to repeat something you've said, don't immediately believe that he/she has difficulty hearing and then start talking louder.

You should ask for clarification before proceeding. You can say something like "I'm sorry. Did I speak too softly or low?"

Do not force a conversation

Everyone would like to believe they have the option of choosing. Therefore, try to not force someone to go in the direction you would like or to do what you want to with a forceful argument. Be aware that persuasion and clear communication are the key to having a productive conversation.

If, for instance, you've made plans with a group of friends to go out but the person has to be dropped out at the last minute due to of a pet-related emergency Don't pressure your friend to continue with the planned outing. Instead, let them know you are disappointed and then act as a good friend by offering assistance.

Chapter 6: Understanding Small Talk

In our modern world, where it is not difficult to have small talk and you'd wish to stay away from it once you've learned the benefits. There are plenty of people who consider small talk as dull or embarrassing and thus would rather not take part in the conversation. This can be on the bus, on a plane or even at the bank or any other place where you are usually disoriented from our surroundings. It is crucial to start by knowing what small talk is before we go into detail about the importance of speaking as a skill for life. When you think of the term "small talk," you should think of it as sharing information about yourself in order that you come across as pleasant.

The reality is it is that making small-talk not as easy as some think, and you realize it once you have to engage in it. The best way to deal with it isn't to avoid it, but instead discover a way to feel at ease when it comes to small talks. I view it to be a crucial aspect that can contribute to a more effective conversation. It's interesting to think about it this way that, many relationships develop through small conversations and we won't be able to tell how close or similar we are with a person until we meet them and learn more about them.

It is important to think of small talk as the brief conversation that you might engage in with someone, or even the occasional stranger, which usually occurs in public spaces. There are times when you believe that there's no reason to participate in a conversation, but I would like to encourage you to give it a shot and you'll be able to feel the satisfaction and satisfaction which comes from it. The reason we should engage in conversation is the fact that we're always near people and have to stay in touch in some way or another.

When I talk about small talk, I am referring to being in a conversation where you don't know our names. This means that you're able to maintain and start an ongoing conversation that is thought to be a great way to communicate. If you're unable to communicate effectively, you don't have to anxiety as it's an interpersonal ability that is easily learned. It will improve your overall health and allow you to live a happier and satisfying life.

A key point to remember about small conversations is that they are not intended to be an obligation, but rather happen naturally. Your goal should not be primarily about making a statement, but rather creating a relaxed environment. There are a myriad of things that could be the basis for an overall discussion. These include music, sports films, etc. In any social or public setting, small conversations help in avoiding anxiety and awkwardness. At first, you may not appreciate its benefits until you've engaged in it, you'll see why conversations are essential to develop life abilities.

In new settings, small talk can assist you build connections, and more importantly, to discover the right voice. Through small talk that we're capable of coexisting as one and assist each other to develop in some way or other. What's more, even an easy thing like talking in a social setting can change your outlook and emotions and help you develop a more positive attitude towards living.

It is your aim to enhance your relationships with others by enhancing your social skills. This start by engaging in conversation. There's nothing to lose by engaging in conversation with a friend and it can be the most effective way to conquer social anxiety. If you are able to acknowledge self-talk, you will be well on your way to gaining as much self-confidence and self-esteem as is possible. Below are some tips to help you excel at small talks:

1)Show your interest: It is crucial that when you engage in self-talk, you show as much enthusiasm as you can to not put off the person you are talking to. Interest is the way an engaging conversation will develop and there is a good chance that you'll have plenty to say. Another crucial aspect is to show that you are interested in others that you appreciate and value the opinions of others. Repeating this frequently will help you more comfortable with self-talk, and you'll begin to enjoy it.

2.) Pose open-ended questions Posing open-ended questions is an essential aspect of having a conversation. This is the only way that both parties are capable of participating in the conversation and will also have the chance to get to know each other better. One aspect of"yes or no" questions is that they usually shut out the thoughts of a person. I'm sure that you realize that open-ended questions lead you to other topics that are interesting and make the conversation more enjoyable.

3)Be an excellent listener Making small talk is one thing but listening is an additional. One must be a great listener to entice the attention of someone else. It shows that you're truly curious about the things they say , and they'll be curious about the things your thoughts are. It also allows you maintain the dialogue when you are aware of what needs been discussed.

4.) body language A small conversation also requires the use of a friendly body language, as it creates an environment of warmth. A proper body language includes engaging in eye contact, looking shoulders at the person you are talking to without moving your arms, etc. This shows them that you're actually engaged in the conversation. It will also help you get in the mood.

5.) Be optimistic: even in the smallest things you should remain positive, especially when you say in the hope to stay clear of any tension. Positive thinking also open your mind and you'll be in a better state to speak. Your partner will be more comfortable speaking with you about a lot.

6)Determine an agreement A further point to remember is that your discussion gains the strength of your conversation only when you can establish an agreement. By doing this, you'll be able to discuss a lot about. When you are asking questions, and ask questions which lead to an agreement. With a common ground, you are able to discuss about issues that interest both sides.

7)Respect the opinions of others To be able to easily engage or talk to people, it's best to start with a sense of respect. It is about respecting what other people have to say instead of simply believing that your words are the only one to be considered. This will put you more likely to build relationships with others and will have fun talking to people, just as much as they do you.

Chapter 7: The Best Way to Engage in Small Talk The Do's and Don'ts

Small talk can be a part of our lives due to a variety of reasons, as we have discussed in previous chapters however, it is crucial to realize that engaging in small talk isn't an extremely difficult job If you are able to figure out how to do doing it without showing any indications of hesitation or fear.

Get ready

It is important to prepare. The majority of people who are smooth talkers are well-prepared on various subjects, which is the reason they have something to discuss. When you go to an interview, at a party or social gathering, take an idea of the topic you'll talk about. Go through the papers or browse news sites online to see what's happening around the world. Try to read and get as much information as you can and take into consideration different opinions on the subject. Avoid researching an area that is controversial, such as politics, because each person has a different opinion and you could be offending some one.

If you're not the type to discuss news, check out the place you're meeting at. Do you find something fascinating about the venue you're going to meet at? Do you know of a fascinating or funny tale that's connected to the location? Explore interesting information about the location and you will be able to be a double-purposed resourceto be a conversation starter, and also show off your knowledge.

A lot of times, people are curious about one others. Tell a humorous or interesting story. Make sure that you don't use inappropriate humor or too intimate. It could be about harmlessly playing prank on a colleague with a wallpaper change on his laptop at work or the time you took a hike and ended up lost. Don't share the sob story about the time your mother died or the time you were raised in foster homes on a string Remember, people prefer positive people, not those who scream and moan every day.

Make a "Top 10 Conversations" or "Top Conversations" List of subjects. Make sure that these topics are ones you're interested in, and you can easily discuss. You should also list five topics that you're not familiar with that you would like to know more about. This will make you appear vulnerable and not seem like you have it all.

If the person doesn't respond in a way that you want, you can try switching subjects. Don't quit after the first attempt that fails. Continue throwing ideas at them until you find something that clicks. Once you have the connection, stay to it for as long as you are able to.

However, don't appear as if you're merely ticking items off of an agenda. Be authentic while keeping the discussion going and open to discussion about issues off your list, too.

Weather

This is among the most common small talk starters you've ever heard however, it is it's one of the more popular ones! You can't think of anything interesting to say? You can fall back on the casual"The weather is just so perfect!" or"I can't believe that it's so cold and it's already April", or"Do you think we'll see our first winter snow anytime soon?" or"I wish it is sunny tomorrowand I'm going to for the beaches "... The possibilities for this are endless!

The weather can change frequently and almost everybody has a different view about the weather, which is why it's very difficult to miss having a discussion about the weather. It's possible to shift the conversation from weather to another matter quite easily without getting too anxious.

If, for instance, you say "I would like to see it sunny tomorrow, I'm going to go for the beaches" You can quickly switch to discussing surfing, the beach, tanning, or a myriad of other topics very effortlessly. It's just a matter of making sure that you leave enough space to continue the conversation.

Act

Some people don't feel comfortable and member of "the crowd" in the sense that they are. It is not uncommon to feel that you're the only one in the crowd and do not want to engage in talk with every person you meet. But the truth is that the strangers may not understand what's going on inside your mind.

The only way out is to be yourself. Consider yourself to be the most popular and important one in the room. Then pretend to be it. Imagine that every person present are your friends and been there to chat with you. It will allow you to meet them and speak to them without hesitation.

You'll appear attractive and radiate an air of friendliness, which makes it much easier for people to talk to you and speak to you. It doesn't mean that you don't have to be you but rather do yourself the best you can. Simply look and feel more accessible - that's the way to go about it. Try this next time you are at an event. You will enjoy yourself and even look forward to the conversations instead of often being dreadful of them.

Mental

Put aside all of your anxieties and doubts. Know that small talk comprises only 5% of what you talk about and around 95 percent in your mind. There's no one who is averse to talking in small talk. All people do, even those who are comfortable in conversation. What is it that sets them apart and is what makes them so popular? First, they are confident in the first step they adopt.

The next time you're in a circumstance where you have to ask your companions to talkwhether it's to begin the conversation, fill in an awkward silence or even end an ongoing conversation, step into. Engage in a confident unimportant conversation. This will make others feel at peace and make you appear to be the hero to them as the person who helped save them from a difficult situation. This will lead to people admiring you, which makes your journey to success little bit more straightforward.

Completion

Who doesn't want to hear positive things about their own self? The answer isn't anyone! We are self-centered and love it when others affirm us in positive ways particularly to our faces!

If you are feeling like your conversation is not flowing or you're trying to create an excellent first impression on someone, praise them. This boost in self-esteem is needed to start conversation. Give it to them and they'll begin to talk with you as if you're your childhood buddies within a matter of minutes.

A few examples of things that you could sayare:

To women:"I truly love the earrings you wear." "When you smile, your face lights up, enhancing your attractiveness." "The lighting brings out the sparkle in your gorgeous eyes."

To men:"You appear to be the man who is able to accomplish anything he puts the effort in." "Of of course, you have been given that raise. A gifted man of your caliber deserves nothing less than the highest."

Generally: "You interior decorating skills are excellent." "You picked the style for this room? It's stunning."

Questions

It is the most effective method to get the conversation moving. Questions are like icebreakers which give people in front of you the impression that you're really curious about what they have to say, which gives confidence to them.

Be sure to not ask any questions that are too private or controversial. You should look for "safe" questions that will keep the conversation moving without creating awkwardness.

A few of the possible questions to ask: "How many years have you been with us for?" "Are you following the college basketball league this season?" "Which EPL soccer team do you prefer?" "How are you familiar with the host?"

Beware of these questions at all cost:"Are you an Republican or an Democrat?" "Who all members of your family are there?" "What project are you currently working for?" "So you are trying to get that job too?" "Why did you and your spouse break up?"

You may be curious, but don't get too much, and definitely be careful not to overstep your boundaries.

Take note

It's a popular misconception that small talk is just about yapping and speaking loudly. Listening is also a crucial part. It is essential to be attentive to what your counterpart has to say. A lot of times we're too busy trying to figure out what we should say next, that we tend to forget the things that someone else is saying.

In addition to being extremely rude, but it can result in your demise. When you listen to other person, you'll immediately be able to come up with ideas and questions while they talk. Responding to and listening helps build relationships between you and your partner in contrast to engaging in one-sided conversations.

Take note of the things they say Particularly the part that is not of interest to you. You may find yourself learning something that is completely new. If you are feeling bored or totally uninterested take yourself into the shoes of their. Do you want people to be distracted and look around, or just give you the blank look (where just one glance indicates that they're not paying attention to what you're speaking)? No, right? You can then offer them the curtsy that you would prefer to receive.

Remember, one-sided talking is referred to as a speech and listening is referred to as a conversation. it is exactly what you need.

Practice having mock conversations at the home of your spouse or your roommate or sibling. It can be difficult to converse with strangers, but preparing beforehand makes sure that you're at the very least prepared for an event that is going to occur.

However, be sure to keep your expectations achievable. If you're not a natural at speaking but you'll never be within a few months. It's a long process, and as we know,"practice is what makes a man (and sometimes even women) the best." Take your time and believe in yourself. As you progress, you will get better Keep practicing.

Humor

Make sure to include a touch of humor into your conversations. If you continue to talk with a heavy heart and are droning on your thoughts, your partner will be distracted and not pay attention to anything you say.

Make a joke from time to time Even if it's at your own cost. Discuss the times your friends or colleagues humorously pranked you. Discuss the embarrassing mistakes you've made that at the time seemed large, but now appear to be an act of ridicule. This will let your friend that you're willing to acknowledge your mistakes, instead of praising them, you decide to take your mistakes with grace Learn from them and continue on to the next stage of your life, leaving them with a the impression that you are a good person.

As previously mentioned Try to keep your comedy clean. Do not engage in unwelcome jokes that could cause a sour taste in your audience or make the situation uncomfortable. Try to avoid bathroom jokes and bedroom jokes. Do not make fun of other people, particularly those in the group or work environment you're at. You don't have a clue about the relationship someone else has with that person. It's okay to make jokes But try to not to be rude towards people.

As an example,"Look at Mr. Simpson dancing and enjoying the moment like no one is watching" is an example of good taste, as in contrast to"Look at Smith making fun of himself in front of the people. After two drinks, Smith is the laughing stock of the evening."

Try Again

Don't give up on the first attempt that fails. There are some who aren't comfortable having conversations with strangers. There are times when you will encounter people who might be monosyllabic and give only just one word or even one sentence responses for your inquiries. Don't take it personally. This isn't you, it's the other person.

There are times when people set out with an intention of having a conversation with a selected group of people, which might exclude you. It could result in them getting distracted and trying to elude themselves from the conversation any chance they have. There is nothing wrong with you They're just not interested.

There are times when people could be suffering from a bad day and do not want to engage in conversation or may even get angry with you. Make them feel sorry for their behavior and then move forward. You're not aware of the struggles they're experiencing and being angry and hurtful will get you nowhere. In fact, it can ruin your mood and make you angry at people.

Small talk is described as being similar to riding the horse. If you are thrown off, you don't shout at the horse , beat your horse by whipping it, or quit completely. You get yourself back up then dust yourself off and move to another horse with the hope of riding it. You will be successful It's just the matter of doing your best.

If you're feeling nervous or uncomfortable approaching individuals Take a deep breath close your eyes, take a deep breath , then affirm to yourself"I can accomplish this."

You, and only you can take care of yourself. If this technique doesn't work, try thismethod:

Find out the reason you are lacking confidence in yourself. Think of the possible reasons and then figure out how to over come them.

Accept that you suffer from low self-esteem. This is the initial step in treating it.

Discuss your issue, this can assist in accepting it. If you can say the issue out loud, it helps make it more real and helps make it easier to accept it.

Consider the good things that have happened to you throughout your life. ask yourself "If I'm not happy, what made these wonderful events occur for my life?" But make sure you consider things that didn't happen on their own however, but as a result of your effort. E.g. receiving a promotion.

Face your fears. Take a step that requires a bit of faith. Don't worry about failing It is the action that is important.

Chapter 8: Minimal Talk in a variety of situations

In general, conversational exchanges are enough to help me form an opinion about an individual. I make quick judgements which are usually completely incorrect, and then abide by the decisions firmly.

Alex Garland - Alex Garland

In the earlier part of the book we have laid out some general guidelines regarding small talks. In this chapter, we'll examine how to apply them to various typical situations. Different settings have distinct types of cultural and social standards. What is acceptable in one context could be considered unacceptable in another. For instance, no one will be able to ignore the fact that an adult swears at a house party for college celebration, but swearing in an office setting could result in unintended consequences. The following segment listeners will be taught the basic rules surrounding small talk are applicable to different aspects of daily life, including the workplace, hair salon weddings, bars and clubs funerals, parties, the first date, corporate meetings or public transportation.

In this moment, you might be asking yourself the need to learn about conversational skills such as in a salon or even at an event. This isn't as significant as the techniques and tips which can apply to other things in your daily life. For instance, if don't want to know about how to conduct a small talk in a hair salon, techniques from this section can be applied to different areas that you are involved in, for instance when someone offers services to you as a whole.

Small conversations at the Workplace

The workplace offers employees numerous opportunities to talk. Lunchtime, breaks, room, or office idle time offer the opportunity for casual, low-risk conversations. Many companies consider the ability to work with others an essential quality. Personal relationships with colleagues personnel can play an important part in determining the extent to which your career can advance. Making friends through casual conversation in the workplace is crucial as employees spend the majority of their time in the company of each other. People who engage in informal conversations should be sure to greet each other with a smile and add some specificity to their inquiries and keep a positive attitude as they discuss neutral subjects and avoid certain topics and adhere to the company's guidelines for conduct.

Begin by greeting your fellow office employees with a friendly greeting. Simple "Hi There!" or "Good morning!" will do. Couple your greeting with smile. Make sure that other employees know you're happy to be with them.

Start the greeting by asking A specific question. In many instances it is advisable to ask "How's doing?" suffices to start small conversation. However, many employees at work meet up with each other several times every week. Thus, a better approach requires more specificity. Consider asking your coworker "How's the day going?" As a result the worker you are asking will have a particular date to reference when responding. Instead of giving a generic answer like "Not terrible," they feel invited to discuss specific details of the specific time frame. In this instance the time period"today" is "today."

In the same vein coworkers might inquire about what you're doing in your work. When they do, try to keep your responses positive and positive. For example, you can respond to a question about your day by saying "It's produced. I completed the document for the meeting tomorrow and am now trying to negotiate an agreement for a new one." It could be tempting to air your frustrations that your work isn't working as intended, or how you did not get an opportunity you had your eye on however, framing your responses in a positive way can boost morale in the workplace. Furthermore, positive attitude shows the ability to manage the stress of a hectic work environment. This can make a the difference between whether or not you are promoted to the position you've been hoping for. Now is the time to think about ways you could reflect on your current circumstances at work and put it in a positive light.

Keep your small talk in the workplace generally neutral. The topics that are neutral will not spark heated debates between coworkers as well as office staff. Some examples of neutral topics are films, television shows and current events, as well as technology, local activities, and plans for the future. When you've got to know your colleagues better and get to know them better, you can change your topics to specific topics which you both have an interest in.

In the earlier chapters of this book, some subjects are not suitable for small conversation. This is particularly relevant in the workplace. There are many topics that can cause conflict and disagreement. They include religion, politics and personal health issues. They also include relationships, and family. Religion and politics naturally have the possibility of controversy. In addition most people think that health concerns, family issues, and relationships are personal matters. Keep the conversation neutral and consider the privacy of those around you.

Finally, offices and other workplaces typically have a written set of rules which loosely regulate the conduct of employees as well as their guests. The establishment usually calls these rules the "code of conduct." Employees who violate rules of conduct will likely be subject to disciplinary actions. This is why employees must be aware of their company's code of conduct in order to ensure that conversations, be it casual or otherwise, are within the rules of behavior.

The workplace offers a wonderful opportunity to practice and improve in small conversations. Engaging in small-talk is an effective in establishing positive relationships with your coworkers. Through greetings that are friendly while remaining positive, talking about non-biased topics and following the rules of conduct, workers are able to build long-lasting friendships as well as social relationships with each other.

Small Chat with a hairdresser

The chair of the hairdresser is one of the areas where conversations are not just encouraged, but is also required. Hairdressers and their clients stay with one another throughout the appointment. Talking about the day's events can help to keep the conversation going and prevents awkward silence. In the salon be thorough talk about local events pay attention to body language, and be sure to enjoy the company of your fellow customers.

In the beginning, when you are making small conversation during a hair styling session, give more details than you normally would. By providing more detail, it will allow both you and your hairdresser more topics to discuss. The client is at the mercy of their hairdresser up to the end time of their appointment. If the conversation drags on or ceases to flow it's not appropriate to close the conversation and break off during the appointment. Thus, you should keep the conversation going. The chair of the hairdresser is a an excellent opportunity to test their conversation skills So, get the most value from it.

The next step is to tailor conversations around local issues. There are many hairdressers who live in the exact area the salon is located, however they will at the very least are in the region. Chances are that they take an notice of the local activities and events. Customers may also learn about upcoming events in the area which they could attend and showcase your new style. The surrounding area provides an opportunity for discussion which both the client and stylist can are able to relate to. If you're a customer who is from out of town tell the stylist. They may be able to suggest interesting local spots to visit.

Also, be sure to be aware of your body communication. Expressions of emotion are a wonderful way to express your emotion and enthusiasm, but stylists use sharp instruments like razors and scissors that could cause you to have a bad haircut, or even more serious an injury. Make sure to keep your gestures to the minimal. Many hairdressers view those who stare at their reflection as being threatening. They might not be looking straight at you, however stylists are able to see your facial expressions through their mirrors. So, try not to roll your eyes at them.

Then, take a break and relax in the company of your hair stylist. Stylists have a conversation with their clients throughout the course of the time they work. Conversations with any client is not an issue for stylists. Keep this in mind. Keep it fun and take advantage of the time at your appointment to practice small talk. Hairdressers have a lot of practice in small talk. When you're not sure, allow them to lead the conversation. If you are worried that you have caused an awkward situation don't be anxious. The hairdresser may forget about it in their discussions with the many clients they meet every day. It occurs to everyone.

When you're making small conversation with your hairdresser, give more information than you would normally concentrate on local happenings make sure you are discerning in your body language and keep in mind that conversation with a hairdresser usually has very little significance.

Small Conversation at the Wedding

Weddings unite people to share a common goal that is to celebrate marriage of a happily married couple. Wedding guests are there to celebrate the newlyweds that invited them. At weddings, there could be instances when socializing is permitted, even when formal celebrations aren't being held. By adhering to the guidelines regarding small talk at weddings, guests may be able to engage in fun conversations at these happy events. Wedding guests need to adapt their body language to the occasion, talk to others, including others, inquire the names of guests who attend, ask questions and be aware of how they behave at the table.

The way you conduct yourself can be a major factor in the way wedding guests view each other. Therefore, it's essential that guests at the wedding be aware of a few tips. First, you must be prepared to interact with other guests. Wedding service manager, James Field, suggests guests make use of the right hand for holding their drinks. This way, they're ready to shake hands when they meet people they haven't met before. Additionally, Field suggests that eye contact is crucial in weddings where people are mingling. Weddings are usually cluttered by distractions, including guests, decorations, pictures food, desserts and even liquor. Make eye contact to show that you're focused at the person in front of you and listening to what they might have to say. Eye contact can also help keep the attention of your partner. Experts suggest keeping eye contact for 60 percent of conversations with one person.

Then, wedding guests, when they find themselves on their own, should seek out others. Begin by contacting the groups with three people or more. Two people in groups could be in an intimate one-on-one discussion. Individual guests might be enthralled by them for the duration of the evening. Larger groups tend to be more welcoming to people more readily. In these gatherings, you should approach them with a smile Introduce yourself and take part in the discussion.

In contrast, if you encounter many people, make sure you be sure to include guests who show an interest in joining the discussion. If a person is new to your group, you can exchange introductions, bring the person up on the subject of discussion and ask the person a question that will encourage them to join in the discussion. You'll look like someone who is social and likes to engage in conversation with other people. In this case, for example, after introducing yourself, you can tell the person who is new to you "Nice for you to get acquainted. We just talked about food in the area. Have you had the chance to try the fish?" This directs the conversation to sharing an experience (remember we've previously discussed having a shared experience and how it could be a great opportunity to get started on small talk) which the newcomer is able to discuss. When you welcome others to join in your conversation, you appear as a person who is social.

If you're stuck for something to discuss talk about the newlyweds. The wedding is all about the couple. Find out if others are in attendance for the bride or groom. (Adjust these terms in a way that is appropriate for couples who are not married and same-sex). There's a fifty-fifty probability that you have the same newlyweds as any other person present in your room. The newlyweds could be shared with guests and creates an interesting topic for discussion.

When you are at a wedding, the possibility of asking conversations can be kept running. The dancing portion of weddings can last to several hours. In this period, many guests are more inclined to be social instead of snoozing in anticipation of the next event. This is why people are often happy to respond to questions that are lighthearted to keep the conversation going. Be prepared to ask questions with an open mindset. Also, be ready to respond to questions. In many situations, asking questions in a large amount is inappropriate, especially when a conversation has taken place. However, in situations where conversation that is extended is encouraged, such as the wedding reception, asking questions can be useful and can help to keep conversations going. If you feel that the person you are talking to would rather stop the conversation However, you can take a jovial exit as well as introduce yourself to the group of at least three.

Also, guests attending the wedding must be aware of the table manners. Wedding planners, working with newlyweds, usually will assign seating to guests at the wedding. So, guests at weddings could be eating with people who aren't even close to each other. The table manners of a wedding dinner dictate that guests refrain from excessive public disclosure, interrupting others or dominating conversations or speaking at an unintentionally high volume. It is important that other guests pay attention to the things you say Don't force them to listen to your talk.

Wedding guests who engage in small talk using the proper body language addressing groups of three or morepeople, inviting other guests to join in the conversation, sharing experiences, revitalising conversations using questions, and demonstrating appropriate table manners will be able to enjoy engaging in conversation during a wedding ceremony that celebrates union and love.

Small Talk in an Bar or a Club

Clubs and bars are, in their nature, a source of social interaction. According to a study from 2012 that was titled Alcohol as well as Group Formation: A Multimodal investigation of the effects of Alcohol on Emotions and Social Bonding A group of researchers conclude that alcohol functions as an agent of social lubrication. The study shows that higher drinking alcohol correlates with a rise in genuine smiles and the amount of time spent talking. Also, the drinking alcohol makes individuals more inclined to engage in conversation with each other. Bar patrons can enhance their social interactions by remembering to be enjoyable time, and also by engaging with others, using a friendly body language, and sharing contact details.

In the first place, patrons of clubs and bars must remember to enjoy themselves. In a club, hanging out with an irritable, serious or angry look suggests that you're not having fun, and you don't have any place that is more important. Bar patrons are likely to avoid those with this type of attitude. If you're simply going to into a bar for one drink on your own, don't follow the guidelines that is provided in this chapter. This book aims to assist readers in improving their social lives through improving their social abilities. Instead, you should play with your acquaintances, give handshakes and high-fives and don't be afraid to make new acquaintances. People visit bar and club to meet new people and enjoy themselves. Find someone they'd like to get to know.

Next, you should include and engage your fellow patrons at the club. It is better to move around the bar than lingering in one place. This Alcohol and Group Formation study also shows that people are more social after drinking. Be social! Socializing is a must in a club or bar. Introduce yourself to others by asking an easy question, such as "How do you feel?" Follow up by making yourself known, and make a comment about the atmosphere. Check out the steps from chapter two for starting small conversations. If you and your companions have an enjoyable and engaging conversation, ask others to participate. Inquire about a topic that is that is relevant to your conversation and follow it up with a discussion of their answer as it is related to the discussion. The conversation could take various unexpected twists as new people join in particularly when alcohol is present. Be prepared for unexpected events, and don't take club conversations too seriously.

However, none of this does not mean that you're an enjoyable person when your body language suggest something else. Be aware of how you can alter your body language in order to communicate the feeling of openness. Relax your arms, check that you're not in a huddle with your group of friends and smile. This shows a desire to befriend new acquaintances.

Last but not least, be sure to make contact with new acquaintances should you desire to get in touch with them again. The exchange of numbers and social media profiles or email addresses provide the new acquaintance with a means to keep in touch with the first encounter. If you think you liked the other bar or club member and wish to speak to them once more, give a positive feedback about the experience, offer reasons for your decision to leave and recommend that you exchange contact details. For instance, you could say "Well I've had great talking to you. I need to return to my buddies today. Do you have an account on Facebook?" An exchange of contact details provides the conversation partners with a means that allows them to further build their relationship the time of their next interaction.

When you are socializing at the bar or in a club make sure you enjoy yourself, engage with people around you, utilize gestures that show social sociability and exchange contact details, if you wish.

Small Talk at an Funeral

Funerals can create sombre moods. There is a lot of emotion, and mourners be unable to come up with the right words. Small talk at funerals is feasible and acceptable, provided it is executed in a professional manner. When you are able to engage in small talk at funerals, show support and be truthful. Do not ask for specific details about the deceased and refrain from making comments that could cause offence to anyone.

Funeral attendees should first be sure to offer words of support to mourners. For instance, a statement such as "I'm sorry for what has happened" is a sign of sympathy and support. Be sure that your tone is reflective of the intention behind it. That is, you should avoid making this statement in a sarcastic or happy attitude. Remember, you're trying to convey your empathy.

If everything else fails, practice integrity. If you are in a bind it's fine to admit it. Funeral guests often struggle with talking due to being overwhelmed by emotion or trying to contain their tears. "I'm not sure what to say" is a good phrase to use in such situations.

Thirdly, do not ask people about their deceased relatives. Don't ask anyone about the death of the deceased or what their favourite memory of the deceased is. Do not inquire what happened to the body after it was discovered. Don't ask about the circumstances. The questions you ask will probably trigger terrible memories associated with the person's passing. If a funeral attendant is willing to divulge the information, without asking to do so, they can do it by themselves and be prepared to provide assistance. Sometimes, simply talking about the issue can help people deal with the loss. But, it's important to not force them to make a decision prior to when they are prepared.

Fourth, be wary of any potentially offensive remarks. Never ever say phrases such as "I am aware of what you are experiencing" or "I am completely aware of how this feels." Everyone grieves the loss of a loved one in a different way. The idea of comparing their experience with yours would be a sham to their personal experiences.

Don't comment about someone's appearance. It is possible to be enticed to tell someone attending a funeral that they look sad to show that you are aware of the person's emotional state. But, remarks like this can make someone feel conscious of their appearance at the time of mourning. Avoid making any comments or inquiries about the attire of funeral attendees.

To summarize, when attending funerals, avoid talking about the details of the funeral. Do not comment on the appearance of anyone which could make people feel self-conscious about their mood. Don't try to connect the incident to your experiences of losing someone you love. Instead, give kind supportive, tender words of encouragement and condolence.

Chapter 9: Talking to Small People for People with Social Anxiety

Social anxiety is a real issue. It could be unfounded or it might not be logical or seem "stupid" however it's there. I am terrified of spiders. Even tiny spiders cause me to scream and then run to the other direction. I'm very fortunate to have a partner who can take care of these spiders on my behalf so that I don't have to worry with them. Or do I? While I am embarrassed to admit it, his having the ability to kill these spiders will ensure that I am afraid of spiders throughout my life.

If I tell you that I'm scared of spiders, they're not just tiny spiders you can find in your bath. I'm not able to look at a photograph of a tarantula, or any spider online (or even worse in videos) with no feeling the shivers rumble through my body, causing an immediate scream , followed by a cover of my eyes. My heart beat increases as my hands begin to sweat, and the feeling of fear is frightening.

Let's say I'm determined to conquer this anxiety. The most harmful thing I could do , and the only thing sure to have my fear a permanent part of my mind for the rest of my life is to take on the biggest prize immediately. In this instance, it is something like being the tarantula. I'm unable to even view the image that shows one in Google or even look at it or even touching one in person! If I were put in this position I'd have an anxiety attack and would not attempt to overcome my fear for a second. It's a terrifying experience.

The same concept applies to the issues you're facing when you are struggling with social anxiety. If you're afraid in social environments, nobody who says "just be yourself" or "come to it and have enjoyable" is going to ease you overcome that. If you follow these people, you could discover yourself in the presence of an ant. It could be a gathering that you do not know anyone or another social gathering where you feel totally disorientated and outside of your comfortable zone. It is important to begin with a small amount of preparation and be prepared. If I'm about to gaze at an actual spider I should know what's taking place so that I can be prepared for it. Surprises aren't fun when they're your biggest fears.

Being alone in a room isn't a problem.

It's not a bad idea to prepare for social situations. Keep in mind that conversation is about your mindset, not about the topic of conversation. That means that you must put yourself in a mindset. It's most convenient to do it at home by yourself, at home. Being in the proper mindset when you're at the center of large-scale celebrations can be an invitation to catastrophe.

This doesn't mean that you have to think about the topics you'll be discussing and how you want to be perceived by others. Of course, you'll have some phrases that you can recall but that's not your only thing you need to think about when preparing. It's about trying to think positive about the event or taking some exercise to lessen your stress about going to the event, or taking an ice bathtub or enjoying peaceful music to help soothe your nerves. Self-care is at the base of everything we do. It is essential to make sure that your time prior to you go to the event needs to be spent calming yourself instead of worrying about how you'll deal with the circumstance. If you are in an optimistic and positive state of mind, you will be more in tune with your emotions and have wonderful conversations. This can also lead to more positive emotions about the people you're likely to meet at the occasion.

Begin with baby steps

The first step in conquering your fear of being afraid is to begin with a degree that is acceptable. Ideally, you'll discover a situation at a social gathering that causes you to feel uncomfortable, but not excessively. If that's not the case and you are in a large party be aware that it's not necessary to have everyone be attentive to you or to be the focus of the celebration in order to be a part of the party. The only thing you have to do is engage in an intimate group. Begin by having one-on-one conversations and gradually move into smaller group discussions. Beware of interacting with a large group for a while because you're only beginning to feel more comfortable. You should stay clear of anything that can make you feel nervous.

When all you've done is talk to a handful of people, that's fantastic. Make sure you celebrate the tiny successes. If you're feeling up for it, then join small groups and employ your body language to take part in conversations. It's about smiling at times, nodding your head and showing that you're listening. You do not need to speak up and everyone will be able to see you as a part in the group. Remember that this was a major move you made to step out of your comfortable zone, so take a moment to thank yourself for it.

Keep in mind the importance of small-talk. It's easy to understand

The great thing of small talk is that you don't need to think to do it too much. Anyone who is in an exchange with someone who have just met realizes that this won't lead to a profound and meaningful point. Everyone knows that conversation is easy and boring. Take advantage of this to ease some stress off. If you're making generic remarks about the space you're in or you're drinking, don't let the negative Nancy inside your head tell you your comments are boring.

Everyone is boring in the beginning. Take a moment and take in the time.

Begin your conversation by making small talk will help you gauge the person's interest during the discussion. If you receive a resounding answer, you're able to continue your conversation. If you receive an answer that is vague with a low-pitched tone, you may utilize any of those escape options that we discussed earlier to escape the situation. Be aware that there is always an exit You've learned how to exit the conversation, so in the event that the situation isn't going as planned there's always a way to protect yourself.

Keep the conversations informal. Don't begin with talking about what you think about space, the government, or the purpose of your life. There are many who don't want to engage in discussions about subjects which require more brain power. Keep in mind that this is only an introduction. You are able to move the conversation in a different direction in the future.

Talk about your fears

While I attended college I had a buddy who was very socially uncomfortable. Therefore, when I demanded going to the college's annual gathering at first, she was disinterested, but then she decided to come along. She arrived looking beautiful in a gorgeous flowing gown. Naturally everyone was eager to talk to her. But she became so nervous that she collapsed in an awkward corner. A friend noticed that she was uncomfortable and approached her and asked if everything was fine. She told her friend that she had been overwhelmed and did not know what to discuss. It was enough for him to carry the conversation to the next level and they had an amazing time at the party. They remain good friends and remain in contact.

When you discuss your fears, you create an emotion of sympathy from the person you are talking to. This makes them want to get to know you better without any discomfort. The thing that often prevents people from speaking up such as, "I am feeling a bit nervous at the moment," or "I get uncomfortable in large crowds" is the anxiety about appearing vulnerable in front of others. The act of expressing our displeasure with certain aspects makes us vulnerable, yet vulnerability can lead to deeper connections.

Get your head out of the way

Be aware that your thoughts during conversations with friends will be your worst enemy if you are suffering from social anxiety. Your thoughts will block out the positive remarks so that you do not speak them out loud, and your thoughts are focused on negative or unwelcome comments you made out loud. An effective way to shut down your internal voice of yours is by speaking to yourself at home. I know this sounds odd but it's true. People who have social anxiety and even introverts like me, have a tendency to think. They are addicted to their heads, and their brain is always analysing and over-thinking. The best method to get rid of the talking banshee that lives in our minds is to talk out loud. It's much more difficult to concentrate when you're talking, so practice speaking by yourself in the mirror at home for two or three minutes at a time until you are used to the sensation of speaking without thinking. A couple of weeks can do wonders for your little talking skills.

Chapter 10: What to Begin A Conversation

How do you make sure you can have amazing conversations with all the people you meet? I've got a few suggestions and tricks for using simple, casual conversations that can lead to amazing and memorable conversations.

A friendly exchange that is well-constructed can make an ordinary conversation amazing. I've divided this article into different types of conversations you might encounter. These casual conversations can to spark a fascinating, deep and insightful discussions with anyone.

Exchanges with friends and family for any situation

It is recommended to start with executioner conversation openers. These are fantastic for engaging in a conversation with another person, or someone you haven't seen in a while. Furthermore, they're definitely more engaging than the usual "Where do you come from?" and "what are you doing?" These are exhausting. Try them.

1. Enlighten me regarding you. This is a remarkable request because it invites another person to divulge information they wish to share. If they want to inform you on their activities it is possible. If they want to teach on their children's behavior They can. Additionally, it's a remarkable way to determine what's going on at the top of a person's mind.

2. Are you taking a shot at anything that is energizing lately? That's my suggestion as opposed to "what are you doing?" If you ask someone if they are engaged in something stimulating will allow the person you are talking to for discussion about something significant in their lives,

instead of just providing you with an exhausting update.

3. What's your tale? This is an interesting and friendly exchange because it allows someone to share an interesting story about them, but there is no way to identify the exciting fact they might share with you.

4. What specific purposeful endeavor would you consider taking to try at the moment? This is among my top suggestions. There is no way to know the mystery side hustle someone is involved in. I am always delighted to hear this request from a person I have in a particular situation which is in line with work but couldn't think of something better than finding out about them through and by.

5. How do you identify who is the host? This can be altered for any kind of event. If you're attending an event, it is recommended that you will share the host

to the best of your ability. If you're attending an administrative or other work event you are able to change the venue. "To how much were you a member of this organization?"

6. What was the highlight of your day? This is an excellent alternative to ask, "how are you?" and provides most intriguing options.

7. What was the most memorable thing about your week? This is a great question to answer instead of the usual question, "How are you?" Or "How's you doing?" It aids people in sharing an optimistic story, rather than simply providing an autopilot response to "Fine" and "Great."

8. Have you attended such an event before? It's possible to change it for a wide variety of events such as Birthday celebrations (did you go to a birthday party last year?) to occasions for systems administration (do you attend every month?).

9. What was the highlight and lowest point of your day until this date? This is a great question when you are a talker. If you're talking to someone who is outgoing, bringing up questions that they can ponder and think about will entice them. The people who are more extroverts enjoy this type of question.

10. Has this been a tumultuous time for you? I usually don't want to know the details of being in a hurry. But, I do use this kind of exchange when someone is a little distracted or is not completely locked into. Sometimes, I am able to recognize the fact that they are busy can draw them.

11. What's the name of that beverage, art work, or game? One of my most-loved setting signs is to get some details on what they are performing or holding. Get information on their wine. Ask if they enjoy the art work they're looking at. Find out if the food they are eating is

acceptable. They are incredibly easy openers.

12. Are you having a blast? An easy way to catch a virus to start is to look for one who isn't with anyone elseand seems to be enjoying themselves. It's nothing but easy to be seated with someone at a table or be seated with someone at the bar , and inquire "Making some amazing memories?" or "Living the dream?" It's a better opener than "How do you feel?"

Keep the conversation going

Okay, these are my 12 executioner openers. Are you interested in getting closer to home? My next plans for exchanges with friends are to help you continue the conversation.

13. What do you plan to do towards the final day of the week? Have you ever had an unexpected interruption in a conversation? The casual exchange is always appreciated. In addition, if it's

either a Tuesday or a Monday it is possible to ask "Did you enjoy yourself during the previous week?" Sometimes, I'll also try, "What's your preferred activity at the end each week?"

14. What are your top restaurants in this area? I frequently ask for personal suggestions. They can be extremely pleasant exchanges. Why? I usually get amazing advice! If someone isn't able to answer your question because they're new to the city, it is possible to discuss where they come from. Win-win!

15. Are you aware of the latest news, sports or television programs in recent times? If you're up to date in sports or news You can also ask whether they are keeping up. If that's the case amazing, then you're sharing many things to all intents and purposes. If not, be sure to inform them!

16. Would you be able to suggest anyone of a kind of mixed drinks/canapes/treats

here? Another way to solicit suggestions is to ask the guests what they would you would like to have or take from the buffet. If they're not eating yet it's possible to get food to share.

17. Everything looks wonderful, but I'm not sure what to buy! What do you think? On the other hand, what have done? The variety of ways to ask for proposals is approaching for advice on how to do. In fact, even at system management events, you are able to go to the bar to ask for suggestions.

18. What a wonderful/cool/revolting/unusual scene. Have you ever been here before? A common thing you'll find in any location you is a place to set. No matter if you're in a home, an restaurant, or a dance venue there will always be something special to discuss and gain some details about.

19. Did you catch that YouTube video with a viral status? It was everywhere in my

online life today. If you have an amazing video you've just seen then bring it up. If they've seen it, you could smile at them. If not it, then show them!

20. I'm making an espresso or going to a bar Do you know of anyone else who have a need for one? This is an amazing idea because of it being able to could make use of it to address a group of people maybe your new group when you are first at your new job or an audience of people you're sitting in a meeting with to make an introduction an event. It's a great way to test the waters and also open up further conversation with those that are along while you are on your coffee run.

If you are unable to resolve the issue If you feel odd when you ask individual questions right from the doorway, make use of your personal situation and environment to start a the discussion. Comment on the food and drinks. Learn more about the area or scene. Additionally, you can inquire about general questions of intrigue such as their favorite games group and YouTube videos.

Make Your Conversation Go to an Even Higher Dimension

We are now ready to begin the deep friendship exchanges.

Perhaps you've been in contact with an individual for a while or perhaps it's someone you've met often before, and you want to talk about more. These are my most intimate friendship exchanges. The book I wrote, Captivate I divide each interaction into three distinct stages. The first 5 minutesThis is your initial introduction, as you get familiar with someone. The first 5 hoursthat is when in which you begin to meet for coffee, collaborating or even having dates. Also, lastly five days of the initial phase are the time where you truly meet friends, accomplices, and even long-term friends.

These questions will assist in moving to the next five hours to the first five days.

21. If you were to pick the character of the form of a film, book or TV show that is a lot like you, which one would you pick? Why? It's a remarkable thing to know if someone has recently spoken about the character on screen, or read or movie. It tells you much about someone's personality to find out what character they think they are.

22. When you were a kid What was your ideal work? Do you think that any part of that is regardless of the circumstances valid? I enjoy asking this question when someone has recently mentioned something from their childhood or growing to be. It also makes you discuss whether your current job is similar to the one they imagined in their childhood.

23. What's your biggest worry? This one is quite profound and soooo wonderful! It typically starts an incredible discussion.

24. What is your most grievous regret? Dissing doubts can really help you in getting acquainted with the person and their past. Perhaps ask if you really want to get familiar with someone!

25. Who is your best model? If you're discussing someone who inspires you who is a chief, a creator or even a huge name, you could have the opportunity to learn an idea of their best model. This is a fantastic way to find out who motivates you too!

Always remember that you must be courageous. You should ask the deep questions. If you're not sincere conversations tend to be based on superficial things. It's energizing to talk about more important aspects within our daily lives. There's a chance that a few of these friendly exchanges may be a bit forward-looking, but when the conversation is moving well, I would encourage you to take a shot. There is no way to tell what you'll discover!

Friendship exchanges on Work-related Topics

The most knowledgeable experts can be productive while working and be friendly. How do you achieve this? It is essential to use the appropriate, respectful exchanges to genuine, open conversations in your workplace. Here are a few additional.

26. Are there any worthy causes you are a part of? Sometimes at work all you discuss concerns... it's... working. This question is awe-inspiring to discover what someone is engaged in outside of work. Make sure you have the best foundation in mind prior to asking for an amazing answer!

27. I'm not sure regarding the _____. Have you have you ever been through this before? The sharing of personal information with others will increase how likable you appear to beand aid in forming new bonds with friends. This is a great way to start a conversation when working with a colleague and also get tips about the

issue you're of today, whether it's another piece of software or a troublesome client.

28. What is the most delightful aspect of working in this office? This is particularly helpful if you're beginning in a new job. It is also a good option if a new person is joining the group and you want to share your personal favorite item to them.

29. Have you received any insider advice regarding working in this area? It is impossible to predict the details you'll hear in this informal exchange! It's an excellent one!

Friendly exchanges to go on an initial Date

You've arranged for your drink and found a nice table. You know the art of tease, but do you know what to talk about when you first meet someone? The most enjoyable exchanges to have for dating will give you an insight into each person you are dating and their character.

30. What job did you have to fulfill as an infant? Perhaps they required to be either a space-traveler or vet. It's possible to follow-up on questions in addition. Are they true to say that they're still interested in space examinations? What changed when they grew into adults. Are they enjoying the sport they're in right now? This type of exchange can lead to opportunities, like future goals and improvement in expertise and more.

31. If you had to choose between one-skydiving or bungee-hopping or scuba jumping, what would you choose? The first question you ask a date is difficult to understand of if your potential date is an Swashbuckler. It could be that they've done at the very least one of these in the past. Perhaps they could be shocked by the possibility of doing one or more of these. Additionally when you're bold positive news: courageous individuals are generally regarded as more attractive? However they'll surely find an amazing

solution as well as an appreciation of the way to deal with a challenge.

32. What's the most important thing I can think of regarding you? When you first meet it is a chance to make yourself more familiar with each other truly. You are trying to determine if someone could be a great match to you (and you are for you). This is a great way to focus on your business.

33. When you were a kid What did you think your life would be now? A great exchange to have with friends to start a date is one that's a Trojan Horse - something light and unpredictable. Actually it's an excellent opportunity for you to relay your expectations to your date, and discuss possible conversations about your early years, your training, or other interests.

34. Which of your family members do you think you are most closely related to? Do you believe that they're especially close to

their parents, their mother or their auntie who is distant? This question gives you an idea of their environment in the family as well as allows them to express themselves as a persona. They could say that they are most like their adoptive parents since they are avid readers or similar to their sister because they have an uncanny comical bent. The people they interact with in their lives is likely giving you an knowledge of the relationship they could be with you.

There are a vast number of wonderful informal exchanges that could be made out on town.

Interesting Conversation Starters

Funny, friendly exchanges could be employed in (nearly) all of these situations and serve only one requirement to make people laugh.

Chuckling is a great way to connect people, and you're bound to become the center of your gathering by participating in some of these enjoyable and fun exchanges.

35. Was there a moment in your life that you experienced an horrendous design mistake? Everybody has at least a few clothes from their past that seemed to be an excellent idea at the time. This casual exchange will help you to become more familiar with the people in your life looked like before you even met them. The exchange will likely follow some incredible stories about their lives as middle-2000s, emotional or 1960s-style. What makes this fun-loving exchange so beneficial is that it is able to cross the divide between ages and bring more mature people out of the crowd to the center of the focus, despite their disregard for social norms from a previous period.

36. What's the most embarrassing incident you've had at school or when you were a kid? This kind of conversation is most effective at gatherings where people be

able to reflect on their own story while laughing at other people sharing their own. Reminiscing to the past may make people feel less calm (so it's a good idea to broadcast the conversation during an extremely stressful day at work).

37. If you could have an unscripted TV show that portrayed the events of your day, which would you name your favorite tune? It's a great way of discussing music , without asking the people which groups they enjoy (which is often uncomfortable and unnatural) as well as it cuts out any unintentional behavior for the sake of having fun. It's a great way to bring the style of a 90s sitcom by looking at people in their gooey bands (which might be a part of their montage extra focus if you ask your friends to offer their own subject music).

38. What do you think of your plan should there be a zombie-like end to the world? You'll be awed by the amount of details

people can put into it when they describe their secret escape, or expanding to escape courses. The fun and friendly exchange could be raucous when you take off each other's Judgment day endurance plans.

This may sound strange but despite discovering some amazing friendly exchanges, make sure to keep it casual and natural. Place these thoughts in the back of your mind for quiet moments in conversation and out of sync silences. Don't try to integrate the conversation into one that usually flows in into a tense manner. Just be yourself, show an intense interest in people who live their lives and then try to learn more about the people you meet.

Chapter 11: Tips to be confident when talking to strangers

Talking with strangers can be like being in the cage of a lion or, even more frighteningly by sticking your head in the mouth of the lion. Certain people experience the sensation of they are suffering from an illness - dry mouth, sweaty palms and trembling, as well as a lost of voice. They may be able to stand up against an army, however, when it comes to speaking to one person they can find their knees becoming soft as butter. To tackle this issue, we must look deeper to find the reason behind it. We all know that finding the root of the issue is the first step towards finding the solution. Here are a few arguments that can justify our hesitation to talk to strangers.

Humans are creatures of nature that require the constant support of other people so they can build their self-confidence. Human evolution may have made fun of individuals in this regard since this pattern makes us dependent on others. Going back to cave and playing with a bat in order to impress women can't be a viable option, therefore we must deal with this problem today. This is the reason why speaking to strangers is a source of fear due to the fear of being rejected and disapproved. They believe that the first interaction won't show their glamor and personality at once and as a result, it is a total fail. Even if a person is clever and smart the anxiety could hinder the ability of the person to speak without mumbling or struggling to speak like a broken gramophone.

I'll ease the anxiety and remind you to know that those who are open and worthy of your consideration are never going to turn you down without giving you another chance. It is impossible to be liked by everyone, and in many cases , it has nothing to do with have to do with how you talk to people when you first meet them. Don't be afraid that your self-esteem could be damaged. Think about the possibility that someone you don't know dislikes your personality after just a few words and decides to turn you down and you don't know why, you'll continue without knowing the person. It's not as if you've lost a lifelong friend. Take this challenge as an opportunity as a normal part of life.

The most effective and powerful instrument you can employ in case you aren't sure where to start is to smile. If you're armed with a smile, and an open heart just an easy "Hi" is enough to get someone to pay at you. People automatically accept each other when they emit positive energy. It's not just about the words you use, but the manner in which you speak it. You may have an excellent opening line however if you're depressed and sneering, nobody will listen to your words. They'll "see" their words.

Fear of rejection is something is eliminated by doing simple exercises. Start by standing before the mirror, and then smile. See how gorgeous you appear when you smile. Smile at everybody you meet even if it's not you who you know them. Smiles are free however it can pay off 10 times over. The smile is the best weapon to increase your confidence level, as the first thing that an individual observes in you is your smile, the conversation will flow easily. Please don't smile in a manner that is disrespectful and any interaction is out of the issue. If you are more cheerful the more easy it will be to engage people you don't know.

It is important to understand that we as people are mirrors. Whatever emotion you express reflect on you. Therefore, your smile can generate a greater positive response, and which will increase your confidence, and you'll not be aware of how the conversation begins on its own.

Another issue you could see when you are talking to someone who isn't knowing what to say the beginning. We all want to go into the conversation with the perfect opening because we think that we'll never get the chance to give an opportunity to make a second impression. It's true to a certain extent. The more general fact is that everyone is distinct and every person is an unique universe. In reality, there is no perfect opener for everyone independently. There are some basic suggestions you can always consider when trying to have a chat with someone who you do not know. Put yourself in the shoes of another and acknowledge that a stranger may feel the same about you. There's a separate section about this, so let's leave this sentence as it is now.

Another reason why you don't have confidence when speaking to strangers is because you're not pretty enough to be able to impress them. Therefore, you may be hesitant to conversation with someone you don't consider because you believe they'll evaluate you based on how you appear, not the words you use. This is an actual fact that eyes have an excellent sense. If your eyes aren't happy with the things they see, likely a conversation is an unproductive one. However, don't believe that you must look like a model to ensure that you're liked and accepted by other people.

The most crucial aspect is to be happy with yourself. Here we can end the circle of self-confidence. To stop it, here's an idea. Meet for a cup of joe with your closest acquaintance, someone you can trust completely and who is always honest and will tell you the truth. There is someone who's like our ever-sleeping conscience.

It's not essential to put on the most trendy clothing, but it is crucial to wear clothes that flatter your physique. An appropriate clothes is the initial step to having confidence in yourself. Consider your friend as a live mirror that will show your weaknesses and positive aspects. When you have decided on your clothes fashion, you'll feel better about your self. It doesn't matter if are short or tall or slim or slender It's dependent on your own personal perception of your self. Your self-esteem will increase and in time, this will be apparent to strangers. This means that half of the battle is won. The next step is to take on the person you've never met with a warm and inviting opening.

In order to cut the lengthy story short, show your best face wear a dress that will make you successful and tell yourself before you leave that you're beautiful and gorgeous and lady luck will guide you.

Ideas for an Effective Opening Line

Lady and gentleman, it is the time is now to find the best opening sentence to start an encounter with a stranger. This isn't rocket science, therefore don't go through a ton of books with promises of a magical outcome. Conversations will not begin on its own and simply watching someone and not speaking to him isn't an alternative. In this situation, you might believe that you've been reading too much "One Flimped Over the Cuckoo's Nest". Here are some ideas to help you get out of awkward situations when you're in a crowd of people you haven't met.

It is always possible to start with "Hi My name is ...". Being able to present yourself in this manner shows you are at ease and are flexible. Keep in mind that you're someone who is not familiar with the person you are defending, and you must give him the time to think before you come in contact with the person. Therefore, if you begin the conversation by saying your name, it's appropriate in the beginning and allows for other issues to be brought up within the dialogue. It is also normal that the person you are talking to will reply by introducing themselves. Always remember to smile. It has proven to be an effective weapon for disarming.

When you meet someone , this is usually the case like an event, party such as a movie, conference etc. It is another topic that anchors you.

You could always add a sentence related to the atmosphere, for instance "What would be a wonderful location to host the celebration, there's nothing better than an evening at the ocean" Or "Don't you feel that the captain of the team contributes in a significant way to the sport?". Although you're with strangers, the situation brought you and is always an opportunity to get started on a conversation regarding the events occurring within you. In the end, this conversation can lead to the next step where you will get to know one another and develop an interesting and perhaps relationship that is heart-to-heart.

If you are planning to meet someone new, take the time to look him over carefully. People's personal accessories reflect their tastes e.g. their jewelry, mobile phones and shoe brand, clothing style.

For instance, if you observe that the subject you are looking at wears Swarovski earrings or an iPhone cellphone, say something about the unique stone cutting method used by Swarovski crystals, or mention that the iPhone is popular this week with the latest model that was introduced in the year before. The first thing to note is that this kind of conversation proves you care about particulars, which can be awe-inspiring to anyone. Secondly it is a sign that you're an intelligent and curious individual. In every case, you'll attract the person of your choice.

A key point to remember here is to not begin talking about things you don't know about. You could end up in an a very awkward situation, and look silly which is not something you wish to do.

If you find yourself in a particular situation with several people There will be the possibility where everyone will make a comment. If you're in a social gathering for instance and someone begins dancing at the dining table, you could begin an exchange by focusing on the individual's attention to this specific incident. At first, everyone will be talking about the incident and laughing. It is not appropriate to start an exchange about the situation. These kinds of events always make for a lively atmosphere to get acquainted with new people. Perhaps each of you might be dancing at the table, too...

It is always possible to discuss the activities that everyone does as well as places where everyone goes. We all go to the movies and discos, bars and galleries, restaurants and so on. It is great that there is a common ground on which everybody feels at home. In order to get people talking, simply link any of these issues to the context you are both in. If, for instance, you spot an attractive person at a film festival, you can begin talking about the top films that were playing in the cinemas prior to the festival. Also, you could discuss a specific movie that was awe-inspiring and share with your friend your thoughts about the film. It is possible to find out through this discussion which kinds of films the person likes, giving you an impression of the kind of person who is against you.

The above topics are hobbies and everyone is more than willing to discuss his passions. It is always possible to keep asking questions about your favourite clubs, artists, actors and art in general etc. But don't create an overflow because the person may be frightened to feel like they're being investigated by police. Therefore, allow them to explain and to talk. Their responses will steer to the next conversation, and you'll be able to decide what questions you should ask next to ensure you don't get stuck in awkward silence.

A friend of mine said that if chat with someone about him and he doesn't get bored, and you'll be the most enjoyable partner. We like to be the subject of conversation. It's always a good idea to inquire about their interests, their profession, and then why they don't have goals and dreams. The more that people speak about their lives, the more they feel like someone is genuinely interested in them. But , be cautious about this as it is not a good idea to overstep the boundaries of privacy.

There are certain private subjects which are not allowed to discuss such as personal healthissues, family issues such as divorce, sexual orientation, divorce (unless the person has shown that they don't want to discuss it) or politics (again should they decide to choose to discuss that subject it is always possible to remain neutral and avoid lengthy debates) economic turmoil (we are already seeing enough of it on the news, television and the internet. Furthermore, it's boring, and does not add to the fun spirit of the conversation) Religion (this is a thorny topic, as everyone has the right to their personal beliefs so don't get into it otherwise your conversation can end quickly and in a bitter way) or diets (you can discuss healthy eating and energy-boosting foods for instance, however the topic of weight loss or diet is subjects which aren't a favorite during the initial meeting).

As you exchange information, you're both revealing your personal interests. So, you need to read between the lines as every word spoken by the other person will be a hint of what to ask or not to ask. Encourage your team to discuss more about their work or interests (if they're excited in it) and then try to identify the common ground. If you notice that you share things in common you can point the similarities using phrases such as "It is so wonderful to find someone you like ...", "How wonderful that we share the same passion in ..."" or "I fully support your view of ..." the subject" or "I am in the same boat about ...". Everyone loves when they meet an ideal soul mate, regardless of whether it's just activities or interests that are similar to fishing for instance.

There are occasions that the person you talk to is talking about something you aren't familiar with. Instead of speaking in the wrong way or worrying about the best way to exit the conversation, just ask them for more details about the subject.

For example, if you inquire about their job and you get a response "I are an IT specialist in web development." Imagine that your web skills increase to include you use your email account and Skype and do some online browsing every now and again and you are not knowledgeable about web-based applications. Instead of standing back, which is unprofessional, ask "Could you elaborate more about the work you do because I'm more of an individual who is financially oriented?".

There's nothing wrong with not being aware of all aspects. There is no need to be an dictionary. In addition, you offer another person an opportunity to demonstrate their abilities, and inspire them to feel proud of their abilities.

If we tell you that you must be a good listener and be able to follow the conversation, it doesn't necessarily mean that your partner is required to have an endless monologue. The first reason is that it's dull and they may think you're aren't interested in the subject. Therefore, be proactive and respond with positive phrases such as "Really what did you do? How did you do it?", "How did you achieve that?" ...?", succeed? "I am impressed by your talents, so please give me more details about ...".

If you notice that the person in front of you is getting worn out you, get involved and continue to talk from your perspective. This gives them an opportunity to learn more about your life experience and take a moment to breathe and take a break. For instance, if you're discussing work and work related issues, you can use phrases similar to "My job is slightly different from yours because I am in the area of ..." or "It is fascinating to learn how other people handle this issue outside of my own business sphere that is ...".

If you observe you are talking about topics the other person isn't keen on, such as arts or sports don't continue to talk about them even though they are your favorites. In the first place, it isn't adding anything to the conversation, and second people will conclude that you're annoying. While you're talking about your most favored football team or your favorite painting, they'll be trying to figure out a way to get away to escape this boring conversation.

Becoming informed of current news stories is an excellent method to maintain a little conversation. One person may have not noticed the fact that Kate Middleton is probably pregnant or the new film "Hobbit" which has caused great excitement and could be interested in these details. If, however, they already know about the information, it's the perfect opportunity to start the conversation going since the two of you have a lot in common as social. Who knows what other things in common between you?

Small talk is a wonderful opportunity to meet one another and provides an opportunity for each of you to consider whether the first meeting can develop into something more. Make sure to be relaxed and natural as everyone enjoys happy people. Even if you don't discuss any vital details, you'll spend quality time together , and you will let the more important things go for the next date.

In simple terms, when you are looking to begin an informal conversation with someone you're not familiar with, firstly, say you name, and greet them. The next step is to recognize the common situation and then adhere to it. You can exchange some personal information and listen to what your partner says, and then ask him questions that will reveal more and more about their lives. If your friend has a more cautious attitude and isn't ready to share about himself, start talking about general subjects like the most recent news stories and eventually the ice will disappear. Be aware of their outfits and compliment them for their style because this is a great method to begin an exchange.

Chapter 12: Get Out and Enjoy The Day

If you've learned the basics It's time to take your skills to the next stage. Everything you require is already in place to you. Go out and learn the techniques, build the abilities, and implement the advice that are provided.

Now is the time to become the seasoned person you're supposed be. Get rid of the old routine and be open to new challenges.

When you've had a bad experience before You can be successful now. The methods you'll learn throughout this publication are easy and effective methods that have been in place throughout the years. The concepts have always been in place, all you had to do was draw on your inner strength to apply them successfully.

They're common sense solutions to everyday problems.

The only thing you're required to do is put in the time! The abilities are already there. They are available. It's just a matter of developing and master them.

There will be obstacles and obstacles, for certain. There isn't a shortcut for improving your skills in conversation. Do not give up when you see difficulty.

Thread into the unknowable.

Engage in social activities whenever you can.

Accept invitations to parties as well as social occasions. It doesn't matter whether you know anyone. Join groups, groups or clubs.

When you are at work, don't be reluctant to work on projects that require you to collaborate with colleagues from different departments and groups.

Opportunities are all around.

If you're on an evening bus trip to your workplace, don't be scared to engage in conversation with your fellow passengers. If you're standing waiting in line to see the barista you love to serve your order, begin an informal conversation with the lady right next to you.

Find a new interest or game. Visit places the places where you can meet people who share your enthusiasm.

Talk to those you are seated with you in the church. Participate in any church activity that bring you to various locations where you will need to meet people.

Don't be afraid to talk to the cashier when shopping for groceries. Also, don't be afraid to speak to the lady who is in the front on you in the banking area.

The possibilities for conversation are limitless. It is inevitable to encounter situations where you can meet new people.

It's time to put aside your fears.

Chapter 13: The Best Ways to Connect with Anyone

Connecting with others means we'll be exposed to different things and, as a result different perceptions. But, it's difficult to make connections with people who we have recently met in the absence of an appraisal process. It's beneficial to have a chance to hear stories from various individuals. Here are the steps that you need to follow in connecting with any person.

Create the Most Impressive Impression

If you are in the presence of a person whom you meet, they judge the person based on their appearance. Your manner of dress, how you present yourself and behavior are the primary factors that the other person is likely to use to judge your character. So, when you initiate an exchange with someone who is not you, they will try to explain their perception of what they perceived about the person at first.

Thus, you need to be impressive and professional to project a positive image to people you've met recently. If you plan to have a chat or eat dinner with someone, you must play the cards effectively.

First, you must employ an effective body language that can display and reflect the way you should be. Be conscious of your movements and tone as well as the expressions. Be enthusiastic and compassionate in the course of your discussion and the manner in which you communicate your message is more important than the words you use. In addition, show the desire to know more and comprehending the person you are talking to. This will help you build trust which is the foundation of any relationship that is successful.

Start an Deep Talk

When we have a conversation with someone who we are not able to handle and we can engage in a conversation that is superficial. We talk about only what we see and the things we are able to see in that moment. If you'd like to get connected with people more often, you must learn to expand beyond the superficial conversations. It is important to provide the other person with an insight into your hobbies and personal preferences. This means that your partner will likely be more willing to discuss their favorite things and interests. But, don't create a personal connection and start uncomfortable and unneeded conversations.

Ask Questions to Get Clarity

It is not enough to be curious about the decisions of another person however, you should also be aware of the reason of your choice. The decision could be based on the political or career stance. Display a desire to know more, without being preoccupied with. At some point, you'll be aware of what you think of the other person without making the conversation personal.

Have the Will to Learn from them

In your discussions be sure to tap into the lives of the person. Make it clear that you are willing to learn more about the individual's experience. Also, don't show the image of dominance talking a lot and making yourself appear more knowledgeable than the other. You can highlight your areas of expertise to demonstrate your abilities but do not try to be bluff. In the end, you'll create an emotional bond and create confidence within the individual. The actor also portrays an absence of pride and is willing to take the lessons learned from another person.

Avoid judging statements

The person you meet may reveal some personal or controversial decision. Don't cause the person to regret revealing his or her identity by asking them sarcastic questions. Instead, demonstrate empathy and positive thoughts about the way the other person approaches to life. Equally important is that if you don't share their views it is important to first demonstrate empathy, and afterward, show your opinion on the subject.

Be Optimistic

There could be disagreements regarding your views as well as those of your counterpart but that shouldn't cause a division. Be sure to recognize any positive aspects of the story of the other. A negative attitude can lead to make the person believe that you are a threat to the self-esteem of the person.

Do not frown.

Try to smile as your body language could influence the topics you need to talk about. A smile indicates that you feel compassion for the person you are talking to and it shows that you are eager to engage. But, make sure you have a large and meaningful smile. It could look awkward if you keep smiling when the other person is going through a painful incident.

Customise Your Discussion

When you first meet at the first meeting, you must ask to learn about the general characteristics of the person you are meeting. Throughout the conversation, make sure to make use of examples and explanations that are in line with the position of the individual. Also, it is recommended to utilize the individual's name when you create an address. If the individual is entitled to the title of professor, doctor or even honourable or honourable, don't forget to include that in the address.

Create an environment that is accommodating

The golden rule says that you must meet the expectations of the person you are competing with. It is possible to share different views however, you don't need to be a critic. Making someone feel comfortable could result in them to be more open and, as a result, you could create intimacy.

Do Not Refrain

Remember, this isn't a debate in which you must prove your belief to be the correct one. Intentional arguing will make the other person feel tired and think that you're trying to reduce their self-esteem. Your position may be acceptable even better in comparison to the other person. However, while standing firm will increase your self-esteem, it does make it difficult to connect with others. So, it is important to get to know the person's feelings and then use your the emotional intelligence to make the right decision.

Don't Be Egocentric

If you are looking to meet more people, it's best to shut away from your own voice. Your self-confidence can prevent your ability to connect with others. However, you need to be honest, but not reveal the gap between you and your new acquaintance. Thus, it is important to get to know the person without critiquing the aspect that is not in line with your beliefs but you must effectively present your viewpoint on certain topics.

Establishing Relationships Through Small Talk

Small talks are the conversation you begin to build a relationship with your family member, friend or business partner. Here are some guidelines about how to talk to the person you wish to meet and the best way to complete the simple task.

Question about the other person

It could be that you're meeting for the first time or maybe, you've met individuals with whom you want to strengthen your relationship with.

Start with General Questions

The primary purpose behind conversation is to establish an atmosphere of intimacy between people. Thus, regardless of the occasion you have met with an individual, you must know them not just as they are but also their thoughts of their preferences, likes, and dislikes. You can inquire about their work, home or the things they're involved in. However when it's an individual, that you might inquire about what they think of your behavior and also make comments on your perception of theirs as well as their interests, reasons they've taken a decision.

At some point, you should ask for more specific Questions

At this stage it is important to be asking more specific and precise questions. You can inquire about previous events or circumstances. You can also inquire about their goals and desires in their lives. However, it is important to ensure that you don't seem to be extremely sensitive.

Don't Create Controversial Discussions

There is a chance that you have distinct backgrounds or opinions. But, discussing the fact in which you have divergent opinions could cause the other person to feel uncomfortable. Instead, you can inquire about the reasons they have chosen to take these opinions, but don't be too focused on the issue. The reasons for the differences could be related to politics, religion or even financial conditions.

If you are asked to answer, use A Clear Language

The use of a vague language also known as colloquial language can make the person who is using it uncomfortable, particularly when they aren't familiar with the language. In the same way, vagueness could cause the meaning not be understood correctly. So, make sure you use full sentences and use clear phrases when answering questions as well as throughout the conversation.

Establishing Instant Rapport Rapport refers to the mutual trust and respect that exists in the relationship. When you first meet someone it is likely that they do really know anything about you. So, in the initial meeting, you need to display the characteristics that can make a first impression. Here are some suggestions regarding how you can conduct yourself in order to establish an immediate connection.

Don't be anxious

You must be comfortable and assume that you have known the person previously and behave as you normally would. Don't fold your hands, but instead your hands should be at your side. The act of folding your hands could indicate that you're defending yourself against insecurity. However keeping your hands at your sides can be a sign of acceptance and ease.

Keep Eye Contact

It is not recommended to shift your attention towards the person in front of you. Take a look at them straight in the eyes. This displays confidence and enthusiasm. But, don't look at the person, but instead focus on them with a calm gaze. Staring at them creates uncertainty and fear and this can make them feel uncomfortable. Conversely maintaining eye contact indicates confidence and you're interested in what you say.

The person's name is used to identify the individual.

The first step in building a strong relationship is to get to know the person. In addition to the specifics that you need to know is the name. Therefore, throughout your conversation, refer to the person you are speaking to by their name. If the person is a professional and you know it, make sure to add the title to the name. For example, the person could be a doctor or professor. Recognizing the achievements of the other person can make them feel proud and be eager to build an association with you. In the absence of acknowledging the accomplishment makes them feel unappreciated and will prevent you in establishing an immediate and lasting relationship.

Do Not Make Your Face Look Wrinkly

The expression of frown is a sign frustration or sadness when you talk to the person you are talking to while smiling who would believe that you are trustworthy? Frowning could also indicate power and aggression. It may be an indication as a sign that you consider the person you are talking to as less than you and that they do not require any special treatment. So, make sure you speak with a smile and be happy about whatever you're talking about. A smile, however, is non-verbal communication, therefore it is important to use it in a manner that is appropriate.

Do not be fooled, nor Do You Need to Forge Your Personality

According to psychologists, the majority of the lies stem from the individual's discontent. The person believes that they are worth more than what have. Thus, they create their identities to conform to the way they think they are. You must be honest and honest when dealing with an individual to establish a rapport instantly.

Also, don't be able to use your successes to intimidate another person.

Healthy Relationships Defined

Current research shows that a large number of people are the victims of relationships that are unhealthy. But, it is made clear when the effects are felt. A healthy relationship promotes equality and fairness. The boundaries and communication are most important factors in an effective relationship.

Communication is the exchange of information between partners. Communication lets partners get a deep understanding of their relationship. A healthy relationship includes the following characteristics of communication:

They are respectful of each other and respect.

Every one of them is able to freely share their thoughts and emotions.

They show compassion for one another by recognizing each other's perspectives without prejudgment.

They exchange information in a way that is mutually beneficial.

They don't engage in blame games.

They are a team that works together towards reaching their goals.

They celebrate their achievements and wins.

Boundaries: Boundaries is a reference to the boundaries that are set in relation to friendship, family as well as time, space and sexuality. In a relationship that is healthy, couples display the following characteristics in relation to boundaries:

The couple allows one another to enjoy time with their family and friends.

They don't monitor the movements of each other; they rather trust each other.

They each give one another room to be themselves and do things that they feel comfortable with.

How to master your relationships

You need to be in control over your relationship, or else it could cause you to be in a bad spot. Here are some suggestions for managing your relationship:

You can control your selection and Connection: Relationships require the people you choose to connect to, so you need to master the art of selecting and connection.

Predict What You Expect from the relationship: Before you begin to build a relationship, you must have a clear set of objectives that you want to accomplish through the relationship.

Be Instinctive: When choosing a person to partner with it is important to follow your gut. Your decision-making process shouldn't be affected by appearances or beliefs of the person you are considering rather, you should follow your intuition. Choose a partner who can be able to work in tandem with you to accomplish your goals, and with whom with whom you have common perceptions.

Concentrate on the Long-Term Goals over short-term situations If you are making goals, it is important to concentrate on long-term accomplishments. Don't judge based on your current circumstances; instead, you should focus consider the potential.

Find out what is necessary to be a healthy relationship: Every commitment has obligations, therefore you must make a list of what you should and shouldn't do within the organization. By examining the requirements, it can help you choose the right partner and help you learn to follow what is required on your own side. In turn, you'll create an enduring relationship that is healthy, with less drama.

Choose the person who meets the above criteria A relationship is meant to last for a long duration, so you must consider making a decision to settle with a partner who can help you grow.

In your relationship, make it clear to your partner What You Should and Should Not Do in Your relationship A majority of relationships fail because of misunderstanding. So, there are some things to avoid when including others in order to make the relationship healthy.

Meet the Essential and Specific needs of the partner according to Your Ability: You must be aware of the needs that your spouse has. But you and your partner must agree on priorities in order to avoid pressures and restrictions in meeting the needs.

Create an environment that makes your partner feel welcome It is possible that there will be some flaws in your partner. It is important to acknowledge and accept the situation; try to find a solution in an understanding and compassionate way.

Innovative Social Wealth Strategies

The social wealth fund is limited amount of money as well as other properties owned by the general public. The wealth is comprised of shares and land that can be utilized to achieve socially beneficial goals.

Advanced Planning

Plans are the strategies are used in pursuit of goals and goals. However the most advanced strategy can be utilized to maximize legal as well as regulatory resources. The advanced planning process will assist you to maximize and protect the value of your net.

It is undisputed that advanced planning has benefits. In fact, there are a variety of ways the tax law and legal system can legitimately be capitalized in order to protect and, in some cases, increase the wealth of individuals. Advanced planning is a great method of structuring capital to protect against claims and offer legal protection against potential complaints:

Wealth Enhancement The method of using sophisticated planning strategies to lower taxes, leading to a greater accumulation of personal wealth. There are a variety of methods that could be employed to boost income. As an example, right utilization of trusts that are charitable could help in maximizing wealth, while also allowing the wealthy to help others in a significant way. The options for those who have a lot of liquidity are the private-placement life insurance, as well as flexible private installments of placement.

Estate Planning The act of making the final disposal of property that is already owned and anticipated to be legally arranged. For the majority of the wealthy easy estate management using methods and financial products like trusts that are backed by credit or traditional insurance is fairly simple and suitable. There are many more sophisticated strategies for those who have more complicated situations, such as self-cancelling statements for instalments and granter-preserved annuity trusts and trusts of marital property that are available for purchase.

The Asset Protection Planning: This is the method of using products to aid in the management of risk and planning techniques for ensuring that the financial wealth of an individual family is not ruined. Certain strategies are very basic and centered on dissociation. The more sophisticated methods of asset protection plan include strategies to transition. Utilizing slave insurance companies in certain instances is also extremely efficient.

Optimizing Social Wealth

Social wealth is the value of all the services you require to meet your social and psychological demands. However Social connection is a the social capital currency.

Social relationships can be described as those with whom you frequently communicate, whether through online platforms, face-to face or via phone, in addition to other ways. These could include members of your family and colleagues, business associates family members, friends, and relatives. Each link has a distinct worth to you. In your view of the social capital total each link contributes in its own way. Stronger connections like close family members as well as close friends for example, take part more than distant acquaintances. The time factor is also a factor and those that you're interfacing with are more active than those who you interact with more.

Another aspect of social connections is that they could be positively or negatively. It is possible to talk with certain individuals, but the same willingness isn't extended to other people. The people that you would like to talk to However, the circumstances that force you to engage with them as a consequence on social duty. The net social capital may be defined as the total of positive connections from which subtract the negative connections.

Social wealth is utilized to satisfy the needs of our emotions, such as protection along with affiliation, security, and network. Social connections having a part in the larger community allows you to feel more prominent than if you were doing things on your own. Certain biological systems have developed as social animals to aid us in maintaining the social connection. This satisfaction system creates a sense happiness. The principal goal of wealth distribution is to supply two things:

Take note of the psychological needs that are result of daily interactions with other people. If you are in contact with people all the time, particularly, those who are interesting to you, and who you are happy with you should be feeling emotional well.

Give confidence in your ability to meet the needs of your emotional self. It's been proven that during situations of emotional turmoil the more social capital you possess the more confident that you will be able to satisfy your emotional desires. It allows you to enjoy your life comfortably and increase your quality of life.

Chapter 14: What to do to Close A Conversation Positively

The art of ending the conversation is as crucial in knowing when to begin it. It is the same for conversations you wish to get rid of. If you think closing a conversation can be just as easy as saying goodbye, it could be more challenging than you imagine particularly when the person you are talking to seems to be truly interested in your.

What is the best time to Stop Small Talk?

Dead air is typically the ideal time to conclude the conversation. An extended, awkward gap in conversation could indicate that you've exhausted the topics to discuss or that the attention of someone else is elsewhere. If someone else appears to be anxious about ending the conversation make sure you do it in a polite manner for them.

You could claim, "I've kept you too long. I'll let you have fun at the celebration," or, "Look at the clock. I've waited too long for you!" Whatever you choose to say, you must demonstrate that you do not wish to invade the privacy of your guest overly, and you don't are determined to get the attention of your guest. It could cause someone else to think that they've behaved rudely, and you might have to tell them that you must leave, particularly if other person states that you're not bothering them at all.

Best Practices to Follow Before You Leave

If you're looking to make an impression that is positive on the person who you meet and make them part of your community It would be an excellent gesture to hand an official business card. If you don't have one on you, then you may provide any information from social media for example, the Facebook user name or your email. You may also request the details of the person you are talking to, in order to are able to reach them when you need to. If you're too worried or uncertain of what to do or how to do it, just wait until they provide alternative options. No matter what, it is practically standard to inquire about contact information after engaging in a lengthy and informal conversation.

Chapter 15: The Way To Leave 'The Party'

Sometimes, we feel embarrassed or even a little embarrassed to inform people that we're about to leave the party most likely because they immediately start asking questions like "Why?", "This is too early?"

The most important thing to be aware of the fact that you live your own life. It is your only chance to live. You are the master of your soul. You have the power to decide the time to go home and how long to remain. You are not your family or friends. ones.

The world is never as black and white as they appear. When you inform someone that you're returning home doesn't mean you can't conduct yourself in a courteous and courteous manner. They may even take you to the parking space. Home is just a way of saying the fact that there's a legitimate reason to return home. It could be because you have a plan for tomorrow or you must get up earlier. Additionally, it could indicate that you're tired and would like to be done with the day.

Why are you leaving for home?

It was a very busy week, and it's best to take some much-needed relaxation. Your celebration is truly amazing however, I'm sorry to say that I must leave.

If you're an introvert, it is important to learn the art of communicating your needs without guilt.

There is no need to give any excuse to anyone. You have your own reasons, and they should accept that or just let it go. It's their issue and not yours.

How to invest in maintaining Connections

When talking, it's easy to think that people are sociable and likeable but the reality is that most of the connections formed through events will fade to obscurity after the conversation has ended. The reason for this is the fact that staying in touch with friends and getting connected to people you meet can be a very demanding and energy-consuming task for introverts.

In this modern age we live in, people don't stay together following a single event or even after a single conversation.

However, I believe it does not always need to be an issue as you could be proactive and make it your responsibility to initiate conversations. To keep your relationships strong it is sometimes necessary to follow up with the new friends we have made at least once every few months. Naturally, I'm not suggesting that you phone everyone you meet at a social gathering but just the people you feel are interesting. People with whom you had fun conversations, and who you considered valuable and would love to make friends with.

Let's say you ran into an acquaintance at a party at home and they got your attention to the point that you instantly dream of having them for dinner someday. The next day, I would suggest messaging them with a smile, saying that you enjoyed their company and thought it was enjoyable. In closing Be clear about your motives by telling them something like "Hopefully I'll meet you sooner rather than later. Cheers!".

Furthermore, it could be certain that you do not have any expectations about the course of your friendship with the person. Make sure your message doesn't appear to be too pushy, needy or emotionally attached. Therefore, based on the assessment you make of someone's personality the possibility is that it will not be appropriate to add the comment about meeting earlier. It's best left up to you discretion.

As in the instance above, if you choose to say it, make sure you're precise and do not sound desperate to be noticed. Most of the time, you shouldn't spend a significant amount of time in chatting with people you do not know. The reason is that even if you're not aware of your time, maybe the person you are talking to is. If you wish to address a couple of questions regarding the shred event, you should do it concisely. But make sure to make sure you are specific. For instance, "Do you care for drinks on Friday?"

The mere desire to keep in touch with someone does not suggest you should spend a lot of money in their lives. The idea is that you could offer them a chance to meet for coffee, go on some time to walk around and perhaps take a drink as you meet up to get to know one another more. There are no commitments.

If after this date, you don't like the person you were with What do you do? You're free to leave at any time.

Positive Social Impact: Two Methods to Motivate Youself to Get Social Today

1. Look your best: display yourself to the world.

I know what you may be thinking at the moment. "Why do you think she would utilize the term Showcase?", "Is she expressing her displeasure with to me?". It's not true, I'm not and I will never be. But before you go any further let me clarify what I refer to as showcase.

When you go to bed at night, if you are at home , and you are asleep, what would you put on? Better yet, what do you wear that you would not want to wear? Ladies don't wear lipsticks, mascara, red foundation, nice dresses and perfume that is good. Men don't wear formal tuxedos or a pair of cuffs. Men are more likely to be typically seen wearing their casual clothes with no shave and not concerned about the smell.

The pictures don't look appealing is it? That's the reason why we do not allow others to view us as they do. In a less appealing light. Even at home, some prefer to stay in their blankets. The reasons for this are clear. In addition our reflection in the mirror makes us less likely to leave and more likely to stay home. In addition to the stack of indulgences, we purchase an unhealthy meal and then go to the movies to fill in the empty space. In addition, we build their waistlines. Familiar picture? Definitely!

There's nothing wrong with taking a break to unwind and recharge your energy. We recognize that life isn't an easy race but rather an endurance race, and it is not necessary to rush to attend a variety of events that you fear every single one of them. Most of the time the notion of attending every single one of these events scares everyone. But it's a different tale when you make staying at home a routine to do the same thing over and over again.

The first step to take is to acknowledge that you're struggling with getting out of your familiar zone. Be honest and don't tell yourself the truth. If you are honest with yourself, you're 40% of the way to healing. This is known as a "recovery" due to the fact that, although a myriad of reasons may be behind your actions however, your actions are putting you down a downward spiral emotionally, physically, and socially. It could be that you are staying in your home to have some time for yourself to recuperate from the effects of the endless socializing you've been involved in recently. Maybe, you're at home because it's become routine?

Conclusion

I hope that this book has been helpful in teaching you improve your confidence in your conversations. I'm sure we've provided you with useful tips to help you to grow your conversations and help you win friends, opportunities and even favors.

Next step, you must take the time to practice. Conversation, no matter if you think of it as a craft or an art form, gets more effective when you do it regularly. To improve your communication skills speak about yourself with the help of a mirror, and pretend to be talking with somebody else. This will teach your body to respond naturally when you engage in conversation.

To improve your listening I would suggest that you listen to music and then repeat it as an unison. This will improve your concentration and help you pay attention more.

Thank you for your kind words and best wishes!

www.ingramcontent.com/pod-product-compliance
Lightning Source LLC
Chambersburg PA
CBHW071839080526
44589CB00012B/1050